I AM A NEW CREATION

BY

HOPE M. BARKER

I AM A NEW CREATION

Copyright © 2022 Hope M. Barker

All rights reserved. No part of this publication may be reproduced, distributed, or transmitted in any form or by any means, including photocopying, recording, or other electronic or mechanical methods, without the prior written permission of the publisher, except in the case of brief quotations embodied in critical reviews and certain other noncommercial uses permitted by copyright law.

ISBN: 978-1-959298-89-2

I AM A NEW CREATION

CONTENTS

CHAPTER ONE	3
CHAPTER TWO	29
CHAPTER THREE	62
CHAPTER FOUR	72
CHAPTER FIVE	115
MORNING LIFE VERSES	151

CHAPTER ONE

On July 18th, 2003, I was driving west on interstate 40, consisting of 3 lanes of traffic both ways, going at about 65 mph toward the mall. It was at that moment when I came up over a knoll and noticed that it looked like traffic had stopped up ahead. I immediately slammed on my brakes which in turn caused them to lock up.

Now for those who have only driven cars with anti-lock braking, the older cars did not have this feature, and if you slammed on the breaks, they could lock up and send your car sliding across the road, significantly increasing your chances of crashing into other cars. It's like driving and hitting a patch of black ice and skating out of control. So here I am, now skating out of control toward 3 lanes of stopped traffic. All I could think was, "I'm going to hit those cars." Everything happened in a blur at 65 miles an hour, out of control. All I could think was, if I could just put my car in the little side lane on the left next to the guard rail, then maybe I could prevent colliding with anyone. All of this happened within split seconds, which is a bit too hard to believe now that I look back at it. I just reacted without really thinking, just instinctively moving. I was almost able to do it; but because my brakes were locked up, my steering wheel would not work like it was supposed to. As I was out of control, I slammed into the guard rail and came in contact with the driver's door. I hit so hard that my vehicle started tipping over to the right. Everything was happening in a glance, and then it felt like I skidded on my right 2 tires toward the guard rail like a pinball. Then I hit on the right side so hard that I tipped back over on my 2 left tires. I then started tipping back and forth from then left and then to my right until I finally settled down on all 4 tires.

At this point, I was in a state of shock; I was hysterical and could not believe that I did not collide with anyone. Apparently, the traffic had not come to a complete stop because I was able to keep moving forward slowly. Immediately, thoughts such as my husband being angry, insurance going up, my car being drivable or not, and if any tires were flat rushed through my head. Then, all I could think about was getting off the interstate to calm down and assess my situation. I saw the Lee Street exit up to my right, and I took it.

Now, this was an area of town that was new to me, so I tried to get to an area where I felt safe enough to stop. Of course, I was driving erratically—I was still very hysterical and crying in fear and relief that no one was harmed. As I write this, I still feel the fear and emotion. I can still experience the accident. It was so indelibly marked on my memory. I will never forget it.

Once I was able to stop and calm down to try to think clearly, I shakily got out of my vehicle. I did a walk around to see if any tires had been flattened and if I could continue to drive it. The only place that I saw damage was to the driver's door. No flat tires, so I thought, "OK," and took a deep breath and tried to stop shaking. Once I had calmed down, I got back into the van and headed back toward my apartment. When I got back, my husband said that a county sheriff had stopped by and left his card and wanted me to call him. He then asked me what had happened. I told him about my collision with the guard rail, and we went out to inspect my van. Again, the only visible damage that we saw was to the driver's side. I then went in and called the number on the county sheriff's card. He then asked me if I had been involved in an accident on Interstate 40, and I told him yes, but since I had only hit a guard rail, I didn't think that I needed to stay on the Interstate. He asked me if I had hit anyone, and I told him no. This confused me because all that I had come in contact with was the guard rail. I told him how amazed I was because I had not hit anyone, and he said ok, and we hung up the phone.

Within approximately 5-10 minutes, 3 county sheriff's cars and 1 state trooper arrived at my apartment. I was shocked to my core! The state trooper came to the door and asked me to come out to his vehicle. I was stunned by the number of officers present and asked what was going on. I then asked, "is this about the guard rail? Did I do something wrong by getting off the highway and coming home?" I didn't understand what was happening. He didn't answer but just asked me to sit in the front seat of his vehicle. I looked at him questioningly. As I write this down, tears are falling, rolling down my face because I can still feel the fear of not knowing what was going on.

I asked him what this was about—did I do something wrong? He then proceeded to ask me questions about my accident. I explained to him what had happened, and then he asked me if I had hit a motorcycle. I said, "of course not!!! I just hit a guard rail. I would have known if I had hit someone." He then proceeded to tell me that I had hit a motorcycle. I couldn't believe it; I did not believe it. I would have felt it or seen it. Just then, one of the county sheriffs stuck his head in the trooper's door and said, in an accusatory tone, "you remember hitting that motorcycle!! You just killed two people!!!"

I looked at him in disbelief and shock, and then I flipped out. I started crying and crying and crying. I could not believe what I was hearing. The trooper asked me if I wanted to change my story, but I was so in shock and disbelief and crying hysterically that I couldn't talk. All I could think about was how was this possible? All I had hit was a guard rail. Two people dead? How? How? How? I don't know what I was saying, if anything, at this point. I just kept crying and crying and crying. Then the 2nd sheriff went to get my husband to try to calm me down. I just didn't –couldn't understand. How did this happen? My husband and the trooper finally got me to calm down, and then he told me that he had to arrest me. I was exhausted and confused and in a daze. He asked me to step out of the car. I was just following instructions at this point. He then told me that he needed to handcuff me. As if in a fog, I stepped out of the car. I was stunned and in shock once more. As if in a nightmare, I got out of the front seat and stood up. He asked me to turn around and place my hands behind my back, and at this, I balked. I said, "Why? I don't understand! I don't believe this! All I did was hit a guard rail! I don't understand!?"

His voice changed, and in a kind and understanding voice, he said, "I'm sorry, Mrs. Barker. I just need you to let me do this." I could see the county sheriff wanting to step in and handcuff me himself. The trooper waved him away and again came toward me, telling me that this just had to be done. At this point, all of the fight went out of me, and I turned around to let him handcuff me. I looked back up at him and asked him where we were going so that my husband would know and could I say goodbye?

He let me. As if in a fog, my husband hugged me, and I leaned into him because my hands were cuffed behind my back. Then the trooper helped me into the back of the trooper's car. I was crying quietly now—just confused, scared, and alone. The place I was always afraid of being—alone. As we drove, I could see the trooper occasionally looking in the rearview to see how I was doing. When we finally pulled into the jail's parking lot, I asked him what was next. I had pretty much cried myself out. You know, I can't remember what he said. He just led me inside—handcuffed with my hands behind my back.

It was not what I expected. I don't know what I expected, but it wasn't this. Here I was, in my skimpy sundress, walking into a narrow area where mostly rough-looking men were. No other women. He took me in the midst of these other men who were also arrested. He then asked me to sit down on a bench, and then he handcuffed me to the bench. I looked around with fear in my eyes. I could see all of those other rough men looking at me, and I asked him to please not leave me alone. He said that he had to do some paperwork but that he would get another officer to watch over me. I can't even put into words the fear in my heart. The chaos around me was so thick that it could be cut with a knife. After what seemed like forever, a plainclothes officer told the officer watching over me to bring me in. There was an office door to the right of where my bench was. As I went in, they seated me next to a desk and asked me to fill out a statement. My mind was so numb that I didn't comprehend what they were asking for, so he got loud and acted like the county sheriff that was so rude and mean to me at my apartment. He said that he wanted me to write down my version of what happened on that piece of paper. As I was writing this down, another plainclothes officer came in, and they started talking to each other. When I had finished, I told them, and he came over and retrieved it and started reading it. Once he finished, he said, "let me tell you what really happened," and proceeded to tell me a different story; the one where he said that I had hit two people on a motorcycle. They tried to confuse me and trip me up, and make me say something other than what I had written down. I asked about the 2 people that the sheriff said died, and they told me that they had not died but were seriously injured and were in the hospital. I started crying and asked why the other officer had said that I had killed them, and he said that they could die at any moment. This made me cry even more. This is when they really got mean. They kept hammering at me, trying to get me to change my story just like you see on TV, but my story did not change because the truth does not change.

After what seemed like forever, the state trooper came back in and could see how rough and mean they were being. He then asked the officer that had been watching over me to come and take me back out to the bench and cuff me again. Once back outside, I asked him what would happen next, and he told me that I had to wait for the judge to hear my statement, and then I would be processed. I didn't know what processed meant, but as I looked around, I felt that I had descended into the pit of hell. I don't know how long this took, but it was approximately 3 hours. Finally, the state trooper came back to tell me that the judge would see me and that I couldn't keep my jewelry. He un-handcuffed me and walked me over to a table. I started crying again, and I asked him if he would please let my husband know what was going on and would he give my jewelry to him. Once again, I asked him how this could be happening to me. I just couldn't comprehend it. He then said in a quiet voice, "Mrs. Barker, I don't understand this either—your bail has been set at a rate that is much higher than it normally is." I started crying harder because he had been the only one who had shown me any human kindness, and I didn't want him to leave me. Of course, he had to, and I thanked him for being kind and for helping me.

As we walked to the room where I would plead not guilty before the Judge, I thanked him once more. He said that he would let my husband know what was going on and give him my jewelry. From that point on, it was like I was on autopilot. Insanity was going on all around me. People were coming in, kicking, spitting, and fighting. People were throwing up and peeing on themselves. It truly was insane. I was finally brought through a door where I was to take my clothes off and be searched, fingerprinted, and put in an orange jumpsuit. I was then placed in another small room where I was no longer handcuffed. It was just big enough for two chairs and a table where a nurse checked my blood pressure and heart rate and then asked several health questions. I was exhausted at this point. Finally, they led me to a cell and told me to take off my orange jumpsuit. At this, I balked! I had seen enough movies on TV about the crazy things that happened, and a new round of fear set in. The female officer rudely ordered me to take it off and put on a paper gown. Again, I balked and asked why and she said, "You are on suicide watch. If you don't take off the jumpsuit, we will help you." They were very big and scary, and by this point, all the fight was gone from me. I took off the orange jumpsuit and put on the paper gown.

As I looked around my surroundings, I saw a metal bunk bed, the toilet/sink combination, and a slit of a window that was up so high that I couldn't see out of it. On the bed was a very thin mattress and a blanket—no sheets or pillow. I was exhausted. As I lay down, all I could think was, how could this be? I slept for a little while but didn't really get any rest. I was tormented by nightmares of my wreck and visions of what would happen to me. When I woke up, I paced around in my cell. It was cold in that paper gown. The air conditioning was on, and I was in shock. I laid back down and pulled the blanket up over my head, and started blowing out my breath, trying to warm up, but I could not get warm. I couldn't go back to sleep because my mind started racing with what-ifs. Fear started taking over. I started losing it, and every now and then, the officer outside the door who had been watching me would yell at me to get quiet and calm down.

Finally, morning came, and I was given soap and a toothbrush. They wanted me to take a shower and led me to the shower room. I cried again as reality set in. Was this how the rest of my life would be spent? As I was led back to my cell, I was given another paper gown. I asked how long I would be like this, and she said that my husband had bonded me out. I asked how long before I could get out, and she said that she didn't know. This only made me more anxious and impatient. After what seemed like forever, the officer opened the door and gave me another orange jumpsuit to put on. She then led me to the area where I had been fingerprinted and photographed. I was given my sundress and sandals and put them on. Once changed, all I could think of was running into my husband's arms and holding him tightly. My mother-in-law had bonded me out with $6500.00 in cash, and she and my husband picked me up in her car. Needless to say, the car ride back to the apartment was a somber one. I felt persecuted once again, the beginning of many days to come.

Once back at the apartment, I immediately wanted to escape my mind. I needed something/anything: alcohol, pills, crack, just something to help me to escape my mind. We went next door and were able to get hooked up with some crack. All fear and anxiety left, and that escape came to me in a giant puff of smoke. This was why I used it – to escape my mind. In another chapter, I'll go into the reasons for my addictions and what caused me to want to escape my mind. I will say this. Crack was the very worst of all my addictions. It was the biggest, ugliest, and worst of all my demons. It was the beginning of the end of my life as I knew it.

The next day was Saturday, with new realities and fears. I started looking through the phone book for lawyers, yet had no money in which to pay one. I'd smoked it all up. And, of course, I couldn't do anything about my situation until Monday, which left me with no drugs for escape. I started flipping out again because there was nothing that I could do at that moment and no way to escape my mind. Finally, Monday came, and I called about going back to work. They told me that I had been fired. I could not understand this. I said, "Isn't a person innocent until proven guilty?" and she just said "No, that it was in all the papers and that I was no longer employed." I was dumbfounded. This just wasn't right or fair. This couldn't be happening. The police had kept my van for evidence, and I no longer had a job. Now, I had a court date coming up, and I didn't know what to do. Everything had spiraled out of control, and I had no way out.

I tried several lawyers and finally found one that we could meet with the next day. Our friend drove us to the lawyer's office and waited while we met with them. After telling my story, they told me that we would have to pay them $25,000.00 in cash up front. This could have just as well be $1 million dollars to me. We had no money. We had smoked up everything we had and had cut most all ties to family in our addiction. This was definitely an impossibility, but the lawyer's assistant said that he would at least go with me to the initial hearing on August 27th. My car wreck had been on July 18th, 2003. This was July 21st, and I had over a month to wait before anything could be done. Now just imagine how it felt to have to wait that long without being able to do anything. This was the beginning of the end. By that Thursday, I found out that the wife who had been on the motorcycle had died and that her husband was still in the hospital. I had truly taken that final step into despair. Satan's fiery darts were penetrating my brain relentlessly, saying, "You piece of #!#* You killed her!! You are nothing but garbage! You don't deserve to live!! You need to die!! You are a murdering crack whore who should have died instead of her!" On and on and on, the fiery darts came. I truly felt like I was insane.

The only time that I could escape those voices in my head was when I could get drunk or high and that only lasted for a little while, and then the voices would come back to yell at me again. I hated who I was and had hated what I had been since I was six years old, and there was nothing that I could do to change my circumstances. I was truly doomed and deserving of my torture. Even though it was an accident, I was still responsible.

Then one night, in the midst of my torment, I happened to look over on the dresser, and I saw my husband's grandmother's Old King James Bible. I thought what the heck, I've never opened one before, but maybe I could find some help or peace in it. You see, I believed in a loving God, not a punishing God, but one who was like this old guy in the sky that you only called upon for important things. I believed in heaven and that if you were good, you would get to go there one day. I didn't believe in Jesus. I just thought that people who did were weird cult people, like the "Moonies" at the airport. These were weak-minded people who couldn't deal with life, and I avoided them at all costs. Like I was really dealing with life—boy, did I have a lot to learn.

Anyway, I saw that Bible and thought, what the heck, I'll give it a try. Well, where do most people start books? In the beginning, and that's where I started reading with all the begets and begots, it made absolutely no sense to me. I closed the book and thought, well at least I gave it a try. You see, something amazing happened when I did this. I was totally unaware of it at the time; but God helped me to realize this later. This was my Revelation 3:20 moment. This is my favorite Scripture in the Bible. It says: "Behold! I stand at the door and knock, if anyone hears my voice and opens the door, I will come in and dine with him and He with Me." What this means to me is, "Hey, Hope, I'm right here waiting for you to ask me to come into your life. I just want to spend time with you and talk and tell you that I'm here for you always." On this night, when I opened the Bible, Jesus was standing at the door, knocking. When I read the Word for the very first time, I was inviting Him in. Even though I didn't realize this at the time, this was the beginning of getting out of the darkness into the light. I was clueless as to what I had done, but I had finally cried out. "If You are real—I need You!" This was my first step toward surrender.

What's so amazing and cool is that this was all it took for me to change. I had tried to change myself for 38 years—since the age of six. I'd hated myself. I hated what my babysitter had done to me and made me become. In trying to change myself, I became that straight "A" student. I was the comedian, I was the people pleaser, and I was the alcoholic and addict. I had tried everything except Jesus. I didn't realize that change was occurring in me, but I did finally fall asleep that night. This was the first good sleep that I had had in a long time. After many more sleepless nights, August 27th finally came. On that morning, I dressed in a suit that I hadn't been able to sell at a 2nd hand store. I was very frightened and apprehensive. After getting dressed, I was trying not to cry, and I happened to look at the TV. VH1 was playing "Calling all Angels" by the group Train. As I listened to the words, I started crying and saying, "I'm calling all angels. I need a sign, God!!" As I write this, I am once again amazed by His amazing love and grace. He's comforting me right now because these memories are just so raw. It's as if it was just yesterday. So here I am crying and writing this book, and God plays this Chris Sligh song called "Still you love me" the words say, "You found me in my darkness, the protector of the weak. I'm emptied out with nothing to offer but still You love me." This is the amazing God that I serve. He comforts me when I need Him. He is so amazing!! Okay, back to the book.

Shortly after that song, our friend drove us to the courthouse around 8 am. We went in, and no assistant lawyer. He had stood me up. I didn't know what I was supposed to do. When they called my name, they said that a continuance had been done. I really didn't know what this meant, so I asked the judge to explain, and he said that the court date had been moved to another day. So we left to go back to the apartment. As we sat waiting for our friend to pick us back up, God sent His Angels to give me the sign that I had asked for. Just then, three of my best friends were walking across the street toward the courthouse. They started walking toward me with arms wide open, and of course, I ran into those outstretched arms. They apologized for being late; the reason was that Julie had overslept, but they didn't realize how on time they really were. There was just a five-minute window for this to occur. Otherwise, we would have missed one another, and I knew that this was my sign. They asked Tommy if it was okay if I went with them. He could see that I really needed them and said that it was okay. Our friend picked him up, and I left with Kim, Betty, and Julie. Once we got in Kim's minivan, they started firing questions at me, saying that they had been searching for me for a long time and that once they saw my picture in the paper, they just knew that they had to find me. They told me how much they loved me, and I just broke down and cried. You see, the devil had lied to me and told me that everyone wanted nothing to do with me. I had just stopped speaking to anyone. I didn't want them to know how far I had fallen, and they did not know about my crack addiction. We had been out of touch for a long time. They assured me how much they loved me and were there for me and always would be. I smile as I write this because this all started because I called out to God for help, and these were my Angels that He sent to get the ball rolling.

We talked about God, and they asked if I was saved. They had always assumed that I was but hadn't ever just asked me directly. I didn't know what they were talking about and when Julie said Jesus, I immediately started blocking what was said. You see, the demons in me were afraid that a seed would be planted, so I immediately shut that conversation down, but I did receive their love and acceptance.

They have stuck with me through thick and thin. I eventually accepted Jesus but not the normal way. The enemy had deceived me about Jesus, so I wouldn't let anyone talk about Him. So Betty had been giving me books to read so that I could escape my mind, and then one day, she gave me a book called "Left Behind." I asked her what it was about and she just said read it; it's a really good book. So I read it and in the back of the book was the "Sinners Prayer." I prayed that prayer, and from that day forward, my life truly began changing from the inside out. My circumstances did not change, but God began to change me. He brought more Christian women into my life to mentor and disciple me. Judy gave me my first Bible. It was the Max Lucado Life Lesson Study Bible. She then introduced me to a Bible study that she and other Christian ladies had on Tuesday nights. She and Sandra would pick me up and take me to church and Bible study. They showed me "Agape" love as I had never known before.

Yet as I write this, I also remember how the enemy hated what was happening and was doing everything in his power to counteract what God was doing. I was still smoking crack, getting drunk, and doing things that would make anyone ashamed. I was still reading the Word; but I was a "babe in Christ," and God had a lot of work to do in me.

This time I prayed before I called and finally found a lawyer who was a Christian and a blessing to me. They had charged me with felony "Hit and Run," and he was only charging me $3000.00, which I could make payments on. This was doable, but right after Thanksgiving, on November 27th, he gave me a call and said that we had to meet right away. This was a very ominous phone call, so we met with him that day. As we waited in the waiting room at the lawyer's office, many thoughts and fears were going through my head; but none would be as bad as the news that he had for me. We sat down at the table, and he just got right down to it. He said, "Hope, I've got some very bad news for you. They have decided to charge you with Second-Degree Murder, Assault with a Deadly Weapon with Malicious Intent to Cause Harm, Felony Hit and Run, and Driving with a Revoked License." I didn't immediately comprehend the first two charges, but I keyed in on the Revoked License charge. I said, "That is not true! My license was not revoked and never has been!" He went on to say that they charged me with it anyway, but this should not be my focus, that I was facing something much, much worse. He said that the Second-Degree Murder charge, along with the three other charges, were being run consecutively and that I was facing up to 50 years in prison.

He also stated that I needed a murder attorney and that there was no way that I could afford one.

I was stunned. I really could not comprehend what he was saying. I asked him to explain run consecutively and he said that each sentence carried a minimum and a maximum prison sentence. When they boxcar them, they go end to end in order to get the maximum prison time. I still couldn't comprehend what he was saying. I looked at Tommy and said, "What does he mean?" Then I started crying, saying, "This just isn't fair. It was an accident!!! My brakes just locked up. I don't understand. What do I do? What can I do?"

John, my lawyer, passed me some Kleenex and said that there was something that he could do. He said that lawyers take turns being court-appointed lawyers. He said that he would go with me to my next trial date and petition the judge to let him be my court-appointed lawyer. Words can't describe what this meant to me. This was a kindness that I did not deserve. I was so very full of gratitude, but I was still so numb that I just couldn't wrap my mind around what was happening.

Once we got home, I spoke to Tommy about it, but he was just as overwhelmed as I was. With the charges that had been placed against me, he just knew that I would be going to prison, and he knew that with my mouth and attitude that I would either be killed or hurt there. This is what he believed, and he told me so. Again, this was shock speaking, so during the week of January 2004; we decided to kill ourselves. I believed that it was for the best; and that God would be okay with it and I would still go to heaven. You see, the enemy knew the Word so much better than this "Baby Christian," and he had me convinced that it would be okay. The holidays were very depressing to us because all we could think about was getting high and escaping the memories of past Christmas' before the crack and the wreck. We looked awful. Tommy had gotten so skinny that he looked like a skeleton with eyes. I couldn't shave my underarms because they were so hollow that I would have cut myself because I had gotten down to 89lbs. We looked like death already, so why not just go ahead and kill ourselves and escape any future suffering. The enemy was having so much fun with us. We decided to die of starvation and dehydration. How very stupid of us. Tommy didn't believe in heaven or God, so he just thought that it would be the end and for the best.

So we tried this for a couple of days, but I could not look at the sink knowing there was water there, and not drink it. I told Tommy that I couldn't do it this way. I asked if there was an easier way? It was the first week of January, and it had been in the teens each night. So he said, "Okay Hope, what we will do is wet ourselves down the next night and then go lay down in the woods and die of hypothermia." This sounded pretty scary to me, but it had to be better than dehydration. But when I woke up the next morning, it was much warmer outside. I spoke to our next door neighbor, and she said that the forecast was calling for 70 degrees that day. I couldn't believe it, and then I got this "knowing" (what Christians call a Rhema) from God. It was like he was saying, "No, my daughter, this is not my plan for you. In fact, Tommy has no intention of committing suicide."

I was hot!!!! All of this insanity, and he had no intention of committing suicide. So I marched right into the apartment and told Tommy that hypothermia was out of the question because it was going to be 70 degrees. I said, "Why don't we just take a straight blade and slit our wrists right now?" (You see, I understood that it was not God's plan, but I couldn't understand Tommy's leading me on that way, and I was mad.) His answer was what God had told me. I just needed to hear it from him, and he said, "Oh, I couldn't do that." This confirmed what God said, which made me even madder. I looked him straight in the eyes and said, "Fine!!

I'll slit your wrists for you, and then I'll slit mine. We'll do it in the bathroom so that we won't make too big a mess." He looked shocked and said, "No, I can't do that either." That's when I decided to take my first "leap of faith." I knew the road ahead of me was going to be very scary, hard, and uncertain, but one thing that I was certain of was that God was real, and I had to start trusting Him. I knew that I couldn't do that and worry about Tommy, so I told him that he had to leave. I told him to call his mom in Martinsville and ask her to pick him up and take him home to live with her. I told him that I had a lot to deal with and that I could not do that with him. I made him call her right then, and he did. She was to come on Sunday, which was the next day, and pick him up.

This was truly one of the hardest things that I have ever done. I'd never been alone. I had pushed everyone away that I loved, and after Sunday, I would be alone for the first time in 42 years. I was scared beyond words, yet I knew that I had to face what was coming my way, and I believed that God would get me through it. The next day, Tommy's mom came to pick him up. I told him that he needed to divorce me because surely Mr.___ would also sue me civilly for money. If we were divorced, he couldn't hurt Tommy or Nana.

As they drove away, I could see my life as I knew it, leaving along with it. I immediately went next door, begging for crack, and because they felt sorry for me, they gave it to me. By that evening, their pity had worn off. No more crack or escape. Prior to Tommy leaving, I had called my nurse friend Betty and had asked if I could go and live in her barn on her farm since we were being kicked out of the apartment, and she had agreed. After I got back to the apartment, I called her and told her that I had sent Tommy to his mom's and that it would just be me. I'm sure that I sounded lost and pitiful. She said that they would be there on Monday to help me move what little stuff I had left. This left me with the rest of the evening and night to "Jones" for more crack, and I realized that I was completely alone.

As I lay in my bed, I started crying uncontrollably. Fear of the unknown started to settle in. Once again, I felt as if I was losing my mind. The enemy was throwing so many lies at me that I just started screaming and crying. I felt so alone!!!!! I needed a hug so very desperately, but I had no one to hug me. I kept screaming and crying, "God, I need a hug! I'm so alone and so scared, and I don't know what to do, and I really just need a hug, but there is no one here to hug me." My 2 cats were in bed with me, and they could tell how distressed I was; they were licking the tears from my face, but they could not hug me, and I was just whimpering, "I just need a hug. I just need a hug. I just need a hug." When all of a sudden, this warm tingle started at my toes, moving up my body, all the way up my body to my head, and then back down again—going up and down and up and down until my whole body was tingling. Then that "peace that surpasses all understanding" came over me, and I realized that I had gotten my hug from the inside out from the Holy Spirit. The Holy Spirit who lived within me had given me my desperately needed hug from the inside out. I then knew that everything was going to be okay. I will never ever forget that moment, and I believe that was when I was "Baptized with the Holy Spirit."

CHAPTER TWO

On Monday, my friends Betty and Charlie came over to help me move. This was the beginning of a new and uncertain chapter in my life. I had no one but God, and I had a lot of scary things coming up. I was truly alone for the first time in 42 years, and I was facing up to 50 years in prison. We packed up what little I had left. Black garbage bags of old clothes that I couldn't take to a 2nd hand store for money. I had already pawned everything else of value for crack. I used to have a nice home and car and jewelry—lots of materialistic things. Now, all I had were these pitiful few bags of nicotine-smelling clothing and a bed, and feelings of loss and loneliness. I looked very pitiful. But my mind and spirit recognized that this was a new start—one with God.

Now I have to describe the barn to you. Betty and Charlie lived in an old farmhouse on tobacco farmland on the outskirts of Elon, North Carolina. If you have ever seen a tobacco barn, you will know exactly what I'm talking about; but if you have never been in one before, I need to describe it to you. This used to be a pack house. The upstairs was for hanging and bundling, and the lower floor was for storage for the market.

Once the tobacco was harvested, the leaves would be placed on sticks and hung from the ceiling to cure for the market; but now it was just a storage place for old junk. Anyway, when we got to Betty's—she told me to place my things upstairs in the farmhouse until I could get the barn habitable. I didn't know what to expect, so we placed my garbage bags there, and then we went to go look at the place where I was going to live. Once inside, I was stunned. You see, I had to clean it out and make it livable before I could stay there. Betty and Charlie were going to let me live upstairs in the farmhouse until I could straighten it out.

This was probably the best idea because I don't think that it would have been good for me to be by myself for a while, and God knew that.

It was a mess. It had years and years of accumulated junk and leftovers from years gone by. There were old tobacco leaves, barrels, old discarded furniture, barbed wire, cabinets, and years and years of old cast-offs. The barn walls had open slits between the old wood allowing the wind to blow through the barn. It was overwhelming, but so were my circumstances; and I had to start somewhere. This was going to be a time of pruning and growing.

Now, remember, it was January 2004, and it was very cold. Charlie loaned me some long johns and coveralls and work boots and gloves. They loved me with tough love. They figured that I had gotten myself into this mess on my own and that I needed to work my way out on my own. They provided shelter and food and encouragement; but not a handout. It was a hand-up, and it was my job to make the barn livable. There was only one electrical outlet and no running water. The first thing on the agenda was to cover the holes in the walls. Betty and Charlie let nothing go to waste, and they had some old, previously used insulation that they had found from another old house. There were rolls and rolls that I could use; so I used a Slammer (an industrial stapler) to start putting up insulation, and in order to do that, I had to move all the junk to the center of the downstairs room. This was a chore in itself. I was not used to doing work like this, but I was determined to make a new life in more ways than one. 2nd Corinthians 5:17 says, "Therefore if any person is in Christ, he is a new creation, the old has passed away. Behold, the fresh and new has come."

I so wanted to be fresh and new. I felt so old and ugly. This barn was exactly what I needed, although this was going to be very hard and painful. I felt like this old and discarded barn that I was renovating—full of old ugly junk and trash that needed to be gotten rid of so that I could fill it up with new and fresh Christ-filled things.

With the help of Charlie, I was able to remove all the junk, and he helped me to wire it with more outlets downstairs and upstairs. I worked very hard, and I cried a lot and yelled a lot and complained a lot and praised a lot, and prayed a lot. I was truly messed up, but I was willing to let God change me. I didn't want to be who I used to be, and because of Christ, I didn't have to be. Actually, this was a healing time for me. The barn was excellent therapy, and I was accomplishing things that I had never done before. This was confidence-building.

Once it was cleaned out and insulated, I then started placing material on the walls, floor, and ceiling. Charlie worked for a manufacturer that made fabric for furniture. Charlie brought home the leftovers and castoffs in large garbage bags. These were in another barn. So once the insulation was done, I started going through the bags and bags of materials—sorting by color and pattern. This was a very monotonous and time-consuming—but healing work. I prayed that God would give me enough material in one color to do the whole downstairs. Don't you know that God answered that prayer? It was the prettiest shade of chestnut, and it fit perfectly. Once again, me and the slammer went to work placing it on the walls, then the floor, and then the ceiling. When it was finished, I truly felt as if I had accomplished something amazing; something that I had done with God's help alone. It's these victories that give us the hope to go on. I had failed at just about everything in my life; but God gave me this sense of accomplishment and victory as encouragement of change and things to come.

Once I finished downstairs, I started upstairs. Now upstairs had a 24-foot ceiling with rafters and a tin roof. Wow– when it rained, you could scream at the top of your lungs and not hear your own voice. I started the process of insulating the walls by using a tall ladder. Of course, I just went up to the rafters but once again accomplished what I had set out to do. In the past, I had started and tried so many things and failed to finish, but here with Christ, I was accomplishing many things, and it felt good.

For upstairs, I chose to do things differently. I chose many different colors and materials so that my walls were like a beautiful patchwork quilt. I smile as I remember this because it was very beautiful and dear to me–just like I was beautiful to God. Piece by piece, I was able to put that barn together; and piece by piece, He was putting me together as well.

Betty and Charlie worked nights, so while I worked during the day, they slept. I would cook and clean for them, not because I had to but because I wanted to. They had given me a second chance, and I was very thankful. In the evenings, before they went to work, we would talk about life and Jesus. On Thursdays, we would do a Bible study with two other women who lived on their road. One of the ladies named Judy started taking me to church, and she gave me my 1st Bible. It was the Max Lucado Life Lesson Study Bible. It changed my life!!!!!

Now I have to say this right now, and I am sure that I will say this again. Jesus saved me, and the Word changed me. You need to get this!! The Word is what changed me. The Word changed my thinking. I had listened to so many lies all my life starting at the age of 6, but finally, I heard the truth, and the "Truth" set me free. It didn't happen overnight, but neither did my downfall. It has been an ongoing process that will not be finished until Jesus returns.

It took me till April to complete the work on the barn. We found old furniture from other barns, and Betty and Amy helped me to make and place curtains on the windows; all 2 of them. This was truly an accomplishment, and I regret not taking pictures because this was a huge part of my recovery and something I would love to show all of you. Anyway, I moved into the barn. This started a new level of growth and healing. This time was a time of pain, anger, tears, and growth. You know when you get saved, you aren't instantly fixed. As I said, that won't happen until He returns and we get those Glorified bodies. Philippians 1:6 (NLT) says, "And I am certain that God, who began the good work within you, will continue His work until it is finally finished on the day when Christ Jesus returns."

I was a train wreck, and I needed a lot of help. I continued to mess up, but our God is a forgiving and loving God. The 1st thing he needed to change in me was to clean up my mouth. I cussed like the worst of sailors. (I could say whole sentences with nothing but cuss words) But God knew how to start with me. He also knew that if He told me all the things that needed to be changed that I would have called it quits right then and there. I would have curled up in a fetal position and said, "I give up." You need to understand something; I was very fragile. Matthew 12:20 says, "A bruised reed shall he not break and a smoldering wick he will not snuff out." I was exactly like that reed and wick. God separated me into only a select few because others would have snuffed out what little flame that I had left. I was so very fragile. I was still an addict and suicidal, and filled with many demons. It wouldn't have taken much from a "Holier than thow" Bible-thumping Pharisee to run me right back to where I came from, and God knew this and He handpicked the people that He placed in my life. You see, He loved me so much just like he loves you.

All I could see was the pain, the sorrow, and the loneliness, but today hindsight truly is 20-20. I have spiritual eyes to see today and to see that he was only working things out for my good and His glory. So, because it was just Him and me in the barn with the select few; I was very lonely. I was used to constant chaos (of my own making), which filled up my every waking moment. The barn was very quiet and lonely. I had no phone, no TV, and no one to talk to except God. One thing I am not is a quiet person, and this was probably one of the hardest adjustments that I had to make because, with the silence, the voices in my head started talking.

I know that now you think that I may be crazy, but everyone has at least 3 voices in their head; theirs, God's, and the enemy's, and my problem was that the enemy's and mine were almost identical. I hated what those voices said to me. There was constant condemnation, constant fear, and constant self-hate. Bad memories would flash in my mind to remind me of all the stupid and awful things that I had done and fear of repeating those things in the future. It was no wonder that I wanted to escape my mind with drugs and alcohol; but those only fed the voices like gasoline to a fire. Things had to change, so my friend Judy gave me a book by Joyce Meyer called "How to Hear From God," and her book was the one that taught me about the 3 voices. She taught me how to discern the difference and how to focus only on God's voice. WOW! WOW! WOW! This was such a breakthrough for me. She taught me to start memorizing scripture so that I could start fighting the lies that the enemy and I told myself so that I could finally start hearing the Truth. I would write down 'life verses' on yellow stickies that Betty had given me and stick them up all over the walls in my barn. When I would start to listen to those voices, I would walk around my barn and start speaking the life verses out loud. This was my 2-edged sword and the beginning of me becoming a "Kick Butt Warrior" for the Lord!!!

Then Judy gave me another book by Max Lucado, and it was called "God Came Near." This book showed me God's heart. You see, I didn't really know anything about God.

He was just this old man in heaven that was in charge of the really important stuff. Not an "up close and personal" kind of God, but when I read "God Came Near," I started to get a different picture of Him.

God is so amazing. He handpicked the people around me and gave me Joyce Meyer as my "Spiritual Mom" and Max Lucado as my "Spiritual Dad," and He gave me the Bible to teach me the truth, and He gave me His Son to save me, and He gave me the Holy Spirit to be my best friend. I was no longer alone, and I was learning to no longer fear being alone. What a revelation! That is what the Word does; it enlightens us and changes us—that's all I really wanted. I didn't want to be who I had become. I just wanted to be loved unconditionally. God was teaching me that I could be changed. I wanted to be who He wanted me to be; I just couldn't figure out how yet. I didn't see who He saw, but I did finally come to understand His love.

Here's a really cool story. While living in the barn- I had been doing yard work and cleaning other Christian friends' houses so that I could have a little money. I still had 2 cats named Callie and Grimmie, and by working odd jobs, I was able to buy cat food, and occasionally I bought beer. I was still an addict and an alcoholic, and I had not been delivered of those things yet. So when I drank, I would chug my "40s" so that I would get drunk quickly and sleep because that's what I did. Well, this was about 6 weeks after Mother's Day. Mother's Day was a bad day for me because I couldn't have children. (In another chapter, I'll explain why) So on Mother's Day, I would get on my pity pot, but on this Mother's Day, both my cats gave birth to kittens. What a gift from God. I loved cats and especially loved kittens. They had been the one constant in my life of chaos. Cats were the closest to the unconditional love that I had ever experienced. Animals don't remind you of all your mistakes and misdeeds. They don't just get up and leave you or turn their backs on you. They just love you. Well, when the kittens were about 6 weeks old, I would put them all on the couch with me, and they would sleep with me and crawl all over me, nuzzling and licking me. I smile as I remember the joy that they brought to me. So, on this day that I was drinking and escaping, I was also journaling. I started crying and asking God why I was still getting drunk. I told Him that I just didn't understand why I did this. Why was I still drinking when I had never known greater peace and joy than when I was in His presence? I just couldn't understand why I was doing this, so God told me that I was trying to run Him off like I had run everyone else off. He said, "Hope, you have been able to run everyone else off because you don't feel that you deserve their love. When your babysitter told you that if anyone ever knew the real you and what you had done, they would never love you and would leave you. You have intentionally sabotaged every friendship and relationship that you have ever had because of what Mike told you when you were six years old. You are now trying to do the same with Me. You think that you will be able to run me off and that I will leave you just like everyone else; but My child, I will never leave you nor forsake you. I love you with a love that is from everlasting to everlasting."

But the old lie from my babysitter was strong, and it just came back, and I just couldn't believe what God was saying to me, and God knew this, so He explained it to me a little differently. He said, "Ok, Hope, you see those little kittens over there. You love them, don't you?" and I said, "Of course, Lord, they are so very precious to me." And He said, "If a big dog came to the door and started to come after them, you would get between the dog and those kittens, and you would protect them and prevent the dog from hurting or killing them, wouldn't you?" And I said "Of course, Lord. I love them," and He said, "And if one of them scratched you while trying to climb your leg or if one of them urinated on your new tennis shoes, would you then just throw them out the door for doing wrong?" And I said, "Of course not, Lord. They are just babies and don't know any better. I love them, I could never do that," and He said, "Well, Hope, I love you like you love those kittens but so, so much more, My child. Do you not understand that no matter what you do, I will always love you and never leave you, no matter what!" And then I finally got it. I finally understood and believed what he said. You see, this was why I was in the barn. This was my "desert time," my time alone with Him.

I have many more amazing stories that I experienced in the barn, but I'll just tell you two more for now. You see, I had been lied to by the devil for so many years that I needed to start understanding the truth. This barn was the place where my blind eyes were being opened. You know that song "Amazing Grace," I never really understood what it meant until I got saved, and then that song was me.

Ok, for the cool stories. Toward the end of the summer, we knew that I would need a source of heat for the winter. Charlie had seen an old wood stove that had been dumped on the side of an old dirt road. We took his truck, and with the help of another neighbor, we loaded that old wood stove up and brought it back to my barn. They put it in my barn and got me a stove pipe and put it together, and wonder of wonders; it worked. Charlie got me some spray paint for the stove pipe, and I spray painted it black, and it looked brand new. So in early October, I was sitting on my porch stoop in from of the barn in a pair of shorts and a t-shirt listening to my radio with headphones that my friend Kim had given me. I listened to K-LOVE, which is a Christian radio station located in the Midwest.

Anyway, I clearly heard God say, "Hope, go get some wood for your wood box." It was empty and was to the right of my porch stoop. So I said, "Ok, God," with a look of like, whatever. I went to get Betty and Charlie's wheelbarrow and ax and headed to the nearby woods and didn't have to go far. I was singing and talking to God out loud and listening to K-LOVE while looking for small pieces of wood. I was half-heartedly looking because it was a very warm day, and I was sweating and getting dusty and dirty. When I had filled the bottom of the wheelbarrow up (because it was an extra-large wheelbarrow), I said, "Ok, God, is this enough wood?" and He said, "No, you need more wood." So I continued to sing and praise Him and gathered more wood. I started getting bigger limbs, and I had to occasionally shorten them up with my ax. I had filled my wheelbarrow up to about half full and stopped and asked, "Is this enough, God?' and He said, "No, you need more wood." Now I was starting to get really warm and sweaty, but I continued on and started looking for bigger pieces because, at that point, I had started to think that maybe this was serious. I was still singing and praising, but I was wondering what was going on. Finally, I had filled my wheelbarrow to 2/3 full and just knew that I had to have enough wood for my wood box. I mean, seriously, I didn't really need any wood yet. It had been a very warm September, and it was early October. Fall here really didn't get cold until November, and it was early October. I was just being obedient because God wanted me to get wood for my wood box. So again, I asked, "Ok, God, now this has to be enough, right?" And He said, "No, you still need more wood." Now, I had reached the point where I was a little irritated, hot, tired, and frustrated. So I said, "Well, God, you are going to have to show me where it is because I have found all that's close by that will fit in my wood stove. So I went back to my barn to change clothes because where He wanted me to go was up under several other old barns. I put on some jeans and a long sleeve shirt because I was going to have to crawl on my belly to get under them. After having changed clothes, I went to the nearest barn and crawled underneath. I found several large, old logs along with several spiders. I prayed for protection from poisonous spiders and snakes because I was very afraid of them but trusted God to protect me. After searching under another barn, I found several more cut logs that would fit in my wood stove, so I exclaimed loudly, " God, this has to be enough, right!?" and He said, "Yes, now go and load your wood stove." So I placed newspapers and cardboard in the bottom and loaded my wood stove for later use. Then I emptied what was left in my wheelbarrow into my wood box and sat down to rest. I lit a cigarette and just wondered what in the heck was going on. I was hot and sweaty and dirty, but my wood stove was ready for a fire.

I heard Charlie moving around in the farmhouse, so I went in and asked him if he had heard anything about us getting some cold weather, and he said, "Yes, it's supposed to get down to 17 degrees tonight," I was amazed. You see, God is Yahweh Yireh (Our Provider), and He knew that I would need every stick of wood that he had me gather to keep warm throughout the night. The old pieces burnt fast and hot and kept me warm. I placed my last stick of wood in the wood stove at 8 am. I had just enough. I didn't know that I needed the wood, but God did. I just had to be obedient and do what He asked. Isn't God amazing?!

My other story concerns my Mom. Now I have to briefly give some background information. When I was six years old, we lived in Martinsville, Virginia, where I was born. My Dad was a school teacher, and my Mom was a nurse. I lived on Augusta Street, and my babysitter lived next door. Every now and then, my babysitter's son, who was 16, would be my babysitter. It was only from when I got off the school bus until mom or Dad got home, but it was at least a couple of hours, and some really horrible things could happen during those 2 hours. You see, he was a pedophile, and he used the words of a six-year-old to blackmail me into doing terrible things. A six-year-old doesn't know how to reason things out. I had made a statement to my friend that he overheard, and he told me that if my parents found out that they would be very angry and punish me and not love me anymore. Of course, I believed him, so once or twice a week over the summer months, he raped me and made me do terrible things that a six-year-old should never be made to do. Finally, toward the end of the summer, he tried to have sex with me up my rectum. I cried and made him stop and told him that I didn't care if he told my parents on me; I was not going to let him do anything more to me. I was still frightened but was adamant. When my mom helped me with my bath that night, she noticed the blood on my rectum and asked me what had happened. When I told her, she said, "What did you do. Did you pull your dress up?" I was stunned. Here I was telling my mom, and what Mike said was being proven. I started denying it and crying, and I told her that I didn't want him to be my babysitter anymore. She said, "We'll see," and that's when I said that I would tell my dad and that he would stop him. And that's when my mom said, "You can't because if you do, he'll kill him and go to prison for the rest of his life." That totally shut me down. What Mike had said was true. I didn't know what to do. I didn't want him to hurt me anymore, but I didn't know how to stop it. I just wanted to die, but I didn't know how to kill myself. A six-year-old doesn't know how to commit suicide, so I just stopped eating. Mom and Dad tried everything to get me to eat, but I didn't want to. They finally took me to my pediatrician, and he prescribed beer to stimulate an appetite which eventually worked. Mike was never my babysitter again, but the damage was done. At the age of six, a lust demon, a lying demon, an eating disorder demon, a depression demon, an addiction demon, and a suicide demon all came into me. I no longer trusted my Mom, and I believed the lie that Mike had told me. "No one will ever love you or want you if they ever find out."

I blocked these memories for many years, but they later resurfaced. Anyway, one night at the barn, I was journaling, and I was crying. I asked God why I was crying, and he said, "Because you don't trust." And I said, "Who don't I trust?" And He said, "You don't trust your mother." And I said, "Of course, I don't trust my mother!" (Remembering back when I was six) And God asked, "Do you trust Me?" And I said, "Of course, I trust you, Lord; You are the only one that I do trust." And He said, "Well, Hope, if I tell you that you can trust your Mother would you believe Me?" And boy, I started getting angry because I could see where God was going with this, so I said, "That's not fair, God! That's not right, you know how I feel. Don't go there!" And He said, "If I tell you that you can trust your Mother would you believe Me?" And I said, "Of course, I would, God. You are the only one that I truly trust. If you put it that way, I have to." And He said, "Hope, you can trust your Mom."

I had always wanted a relationship like other girls had with their moms, a close, loving relationship, but the devil (through Mike) had prevented that from happening. Now God was telling me that I could trust my Mom. I started celebrating right there in the barn by dancing and singing, and praising God. Once I finally sat back down and got quiet, I heard a knocking on my barn door. I opened the door and, wonder of wonders; there was my Mom. I walked right into her arms and hugged her tightly. My mom lived in Roanoke, Virginia, and I was living in North Carolina. I had not seen her in over a year and had not been in contact with her. You see, God's timing is perfect. That conversation was timed perfectly and divinely. If my Mom had knocked on the door before God and I had had our conversation, I would not have let her in the door. If she had knocked 30 minutes after our conversation, I would have let her in, but I would not have walked into her arms' but because it was right after our conversation; He set us both up for the relationship that I had always wanted.

You see, the devil hates love and family, and he will do everything that he can to destroy them. She lived in Virginia, and here I was in a barn in North Carolina. This was a total surprise, but God is love and the restorer of family. Once again, isn't God amazing!?

By October, my husband had moved to Oak Island, North Carolina, with a friend. We had attempted to be together, but addiction continued to be a problem. By November, he asked me to move there with him. He had gotten a job at a local store and was also doing plumbing work with our friend that he was living with. I moved down by the end of November. The only problem was that I was saved, and he wasn't. We were both trying to get clean, but we were our own worst enemies. Whenever he tried to quit, I wanted some crack, and when I tried to quit, he wanted some crack. Even when we both wanted to quit together, people would just show up with it. That's how the enemy works. When you want it, you can't find it, but when you are trying to quit, someone wakes you up with a crack pipe at 3 am and lights it. You can't say no.

Now don't get me wrong, this wasn't how it always was. Many wonderful things were also happening. I continued to read the Word, pray, and grow. I was still an addict and full of many demons, but God was working on me. Oak Island was one of the sweetest gifts that God could have given me. You see, I love the ocean, and it is my favorite place in the world. God knew what I would be getting ready to face, so he blessed me with the gift of the beach for 9 whole months before going to prison. I was still getting drunk, and I still got high, but God was working on me. I kept falling down, but I also kept getting back up. That's all God asks us to do. Just ask for forgiveness and get back up and try again. You see, He knows our hearts.

Tommy took me to several churches on the Island, but none were right for me.

I had prayed for God's best church for me, one that would be a blessing to me and one that I, too, could bless. I had also been praying for a Christian friend and mentor to spend time with and grow with. I continued to look, but there was nothing within walking or bike riding distance. Every time we went by this church in Shallotte that was 45 minutes away, I would get my Holy Spirit hug, and I knew that it was my church, and I would say, "That's my church!" but I knew that I couldn't drive and I had no way to get there. Tommy didn't understand how much I needed a "Home" church. But by the first of the year, he finally understood how important it was to me, and he took me there. You see, he loved me very much, he didn't understand what I was looking for, but he wanted to please me and make me happy. When we pulled into the Highest Praise parking lot, I got very excited. When we walked through the door, I got a full-body Holy Spirit Hug. I knew that I had found my church home. It was wonderful. It was an answered prayer, and it was more than I could imagine. It was a Pentecostal, hand raising, Lord praising, dancing, singing, Bible-based, have a good time kind of church.

The only problem was that I knew that Tommy wouldn't want to go every Sunday, and I wanted to go every Sunday and Wednesday (for Bible study). He saw how much it meant to me and brought me back the next Sunday, but I knew that God had to do something in order to get me there every Sunday.

I called the church office to see if there was anyone who lived on the Island that could take me there. They said that there were several people and that they would introduce me on the next Sunday, so I pleaded and begged Tommy to take me for a 3rd Sunday. He did, and I was introduced to this woman that I had seen sitting up front. She was a very charismatic Christian. Her name was Joanna, and she lived on the Island, not 7 houses from where I was living. Now, how cool is that. Not only that, but she became the Christian mentor and friend that I had prayed for and was everything and more than I could have asked for. Isn't God the Coolest God Ever?! She called me "Hopie," a term of endearment that my dad had used for me, and it was and still is a very special name to me. We were perfect for each other. She taught me so very much, and I will always be indebted to her for taking me under her wing. Every time the church doors were open, we were there. Her children went to the school that they had there, and I got to know others there quickly. This was the first church that I had ever joined, and I got Water Baptized there. I also got to be in a play called Heavens Gates/Hells Flames. I was an angel, and it meant so very much to me to be a part of God's family.

My time on Oak Island was a blessing, but that doesn't mean that everything was wonderful and I was living right. I was still a very sick person. I was still an addict and alcoholic. I was still a liar, and I was a thief. I was still running from myself and my actions, but I was also running to God. During this time, I learned so many things. I was reading the Word every day, and I was going to my friend Joanna's for wisdom and knowledge. I was praying and speaking forth my deliverance as Joyce Meyer had taught me. I would say, "Thank you, Lord, for delivering me of all my addictions." I had started saying this while in the barn because my friend Judy had given me a book called "Me and My Big Mouth" by Joyce Meyer. In it, I learned that "There was life and death in the power of the tongue." This is from Proverbs 18:21. I learned to speak forth life instead of death. I was also reading books by Max Lucado, and I got up early and watched the Shepherds Chapel with Pastor Arnold Murrey. I was so messed up, but I was trying, and once again, that's all God asks us to do. The Word says in

Galatians 6:9 (NLT), "So let's not get tired of doing what is good. At just the right time we will reap a harvest of blessing if we don't give up."

What that means to me is to keep on trying. You see, while in these flesh bodies, we will never be perfect. We just need to ask for forgiveness and mean it, then get back up and try again. This is the pattern God uses. Once we get over the first hurdle, He places the next one before us. This will continue until we meet Jesus and get our "Glorified bodies." "There is no one perfect, no not one." He is working on all of us; just some like me have a whole lot to work on.

Now I have 3 cool stories to tell while on Oak Island. I actually have many, but I would be writing forever because God is just that cool—El Sababa Olam. The Coolest God Ever!!!!

Okay, the 1st story: Not every day but at least 3 times a week, I would buy or steal a couple of 40's—that's 40oz beers. I would get the "Ice" kind because it was a higher alcohol content. I would then go to the beach and chug them for a quick drunk. On one of these days; I was looking out at the ocean, and the "enemy" said, "You don't want to go to prison. Why do you even keep trying? You are never going to get better. Why don't you just start swimming out in the ocean as far as you can until you can't swim any farther so that you can't swim back? You'll just drown, and the sharks will eat you, and you won't be a problem for anyone anymore."

I knew whose voice this was, but I also knew that even if I did this, "I could not be snatched from God's hand" John 10:29. That I was His and killing myself would not change that. You see, I had had a spirit of suicide in me since I was six. So I spoke out loud to God, no one else was on the beach. "God! Why does the enemy want me to do this? I know that I'm Yours, and he can't snatch me from Your hand, so why does he want me to do this?" God said, "If he can stop you by taking your life, then you won't be able to do the things that I created you to do or reach the people that I created you to reach." This made sense to me, so I told my friend Joanna, and we called the Pastor and set up an appointment to talk to him. We prayed, and he anointed me with oil, and I was delivered of that spirit of suicide that day! Hallelujah!! Don't we serve an AWESOME GOD!!!

Story #2: I was still smoking crack cocaine: but I was trying to quit. Every day I would say, "I'm not going to smoke crack today," but it was like every time I tried to quit, someone would come home with it. Then I would smoke it and feel guilty and ashamed, and I would run and hide from God just like Adam and Eve. The 1st time I made it to 2 weeks of being clean and then failed, and I hid from God by not talking to Him or reading the Word and just hated myself for about 5 days. Then, I would run back to Him and repent. Then I would smoke again and hide from Him again, but only hid from Him for about 3 days. Then I would run back, repenting. Finally, I got to where I was lighting the pipe and calling to Him for help. This was a very profound moment for me. He wanted me to stop running from Him and to start running to Him. He saw me whether I was hiding from Him or not. He knew where I was and what I was doing, and He loved me anyway; but He couldn't help me if I was running from Him—I had to run to Him. He helped me even while I was lighting that crack pipe. I learned to seek Him in the midst of my sin. There is a phrase that says, "come as you are." We can't get help unless we come as we are. Jesus said, and I'm paraphrasing, "I didn't come to save the well, I came to save the sick." Mark 2:17.

STOP running from Him and start running to Him. It's the only way that you will get well.

Finally, for my 3rd story: I was reading a book by Joyce Meyer about the Spiritual Gifts. God had been putting a desire in my heart for the Gift of my Prayer Tongue. Now there are two types of praying in tongues. The 1st is the Gift of Tongues, where you speak out in church, and someone interprets it. The other gift is your Prayer Tongue. This is the one the Holy Spirit had been nudging me to ask for. You see, your prayer tongue is allowing, through utterances and groans and words, the Holy Spirit to pray for you what you need most. Most of the time, our finite minds don't know what to pray for, but the Holy Spirit knows just what we need. When you pray in your Prayer Tongue, He prays for exactly what is needed.

Well, Joyce had just explained this in the book that I was reading, so I asked God for this gift. I started letting the Holy Spirit make an utterance that sounded to me like gibberish coming out of my mouth. Immediately the enemy started saying, "You are just crazy!! You are speaking gibberish! Your window is wide open, and if someone walks by and hears you, they are going to think that you are crazy, and they will lock you up and throw away the key!"

I listened to the enemy and believed it. Then I said to God, "Well, God, I guess that now is not the right time for me to have this gift; so when You are ready to give it to me, just let me know." I then decided to go visit my friend Joanna. She mentored and taught me about Jesus, and I helped her to clean her house. She had 4 children and could always use a helping hand, and I liked to clean, so we helped one another out. I walked into her house and sat at the dining room table while her children were getting ready for school, and I started helping to clean the table—just talking about life and normal things. I didn't mention the praying in tongues thing. I hadn't spoken to anyone about it. It was just between God and me. Well, out of nowhere, she says, "Hopie, the Holy Spirit just told me that God wants you to have your Prayer Tongue." My eyes got as big as silver dollars, my mouth dropped open, and I was speechless. I couldn't believe it. I was awestruck. I told her what had just happened prior to my coming over, and she told me that the devil didn't want me to have this gift. You see, Satan can't understand our Prayer Tongue, and he hates when we pray in tongues because he can't attempt to counteract our prayers because he can't understand what we are saying. It's a very powerful weapon.

She then told me to try again and that she would stand in the Gap for me while I received my Prayer Tongue. So once again, I allowed the Holy Spirit to pray through me.

The words started coming out of my mouth. It was like I was speaking another language. I didn't know what I was saying, but I knew that this was my Prayer Tongue. She then said, "Hopie, the Holy Spirit wants you to know God's special name for you. Ask Him to tell you. The next word that came out of my mouth was Kouish. The Holy Spirit gave her the interpretation, and she told me that Kouish means beautiful.

I just started crying. You see, I had felt so ugly for so long, not only on the inside but on the outside too. I was skinny, my hair was thin and short, and I had missing teeth, and for God to call me beautiful meant the world to me. I tear up even now as I write this because I'll never forget how precious He made me feel that day. I'll never ever forget it; from ashes to beauty.

We praised and hugged and danced around because He is just so loving and kind. As I was leaving to go back home, she told me to practice allowing the Holy Spirit to pray through me and to do it frequently so that the enemy could not steal it again. So I did. I even sang in tongues. Of course, the enemy tried to steal it by saying that I was crazy or that I was just making up words; but I fought him by rebuking him in the Name of Jesus and by thanking God for the Gift of my Prayer Tongue. God has given me so many gifts—Jesus being the most precious.

I'm sure that my story isn't very different from many others; but I'm sharing my story so that others will understand, "The thief comes to steal, kill, and destroy; but Jesus came that we may have life and have it abundantly" John 10:10. I was almost completely destroyed. The enemy stole my childhood, my peace, and my joy, and because of it, He almost took my life, BUT GOD showed up and showed out!! The Word says in Psalm 139 (my favorite psalm), "How precious are Your Thoughts to me, O God! How great is the sum of them! If I should count them, they would be more in number than the grains of the sand." I couldn't comprehend that His thoughts could be more than all the grains of the sand. You see, when I first read this, I just thought about all the sand on the beach, but He didn't just mean that. When He talks of sand, he means all the sand on the beach, all the sand on the floors of the oceans, and all the sand of the desert. That's way more than I can wrap my mind around. I just couldn't comprehend this, so I asked Him to explain it to me, and you know, of course, He did.

This is how He explained it to me. I had a coffee table, and he told me to imagine a line starting on one end of the coffee table and ending on the other end. He then said to imagine that this coffee table was my world and life. It was a 3-dimensional world, but I was bound by time, and He was not. By being bound by time, I mean that I was born on 3-6-1961 and that at this time I was 43 years old. On the table, I was about mid-way across; but God was not bound by time. He could walk all around the table of my life. He could watch my birth for a thousand years. He could see my car wreck and plan for the right lawyer, place the right people in my path to mentor me, He could spend years and years on how to develop my faith—(More thoughts toward me than the grains of sand). I could finally understand it, and I was amazed by it because it really proved how much He really loves me. He hears me when I talk to Him. He sings over me while I sleep; and He waits with excited expectation for me to try to understand Him and His love.

CHAPTER THREE

As I previously stated, my car accident occurred on July 18, 2003. I was first charged with Felony Hit & Run, but on Nov 27th, I found out that I was also being charged with 2nd-degree murder, assault with a deadly weapon with malicious intent to cause harm, and driving with a revoked license. They had run them consecutively, so I was facing up to 50 years in prison. At the time, I could only focus on driving with a revoked license. My license had not been revoked at the time of the accident, but the "powers that be" were able to add this after the fact due to an unpaid seatbelt conviction to make me look much worse to the jury. I focused on this because the rest was more than my mind could handle at the time. My lawyer tried to reign me back in, but I was in such a fog that I just couldn't comprehend it all because it made no sense. All I could keep thinking was that it was just an accident. Every time I thought about the woman who died- I would flip out and cry uncontrollably. The only relief that I could find was escaping through drugs and alcohol, but a new peace had started through reading psalms out loud; I didn't understand it, but it helped me.

Anyway, as I previously have written, I was out on bond and spent the next 2 years at the barn and on Oak Island while Mr ___'s lawyer was trying to prove that I had been out driving without brakes with malicious intent to kill people. This was crazy because I had brakes—just not the best ones. I did have a leak in my brake fluid, and I would have to add fluid frequently- but I was not a car mechanic, and brakes were not at the top of my list of purchases at the time. I'm just being honest. I had traded all of my previous good cars for crack and was left with this old, beat-up Toyota van. For this, I do take responsibility. If my brakes had been better, if I had not been a crack addict, if I had not been on the road that day, then Mrs.___ would not be dead. For this, I will be eternally sorry. At this moment, while writing, I am again feeling the sorrow that I was responsible for the death of another person. I will never be able to take away the pain and sorrow that I caused by this accident. It took me 4 years just to come to terms with it, and then the Holy Spirit gave me peace.

You see, Mrs.___ was a Christian. The Holy Spirit told me that I was a "Crown" for her. As a "Baby Christian," I thought that the crowns spoken of in the bible were made of gold and silver; but the Holy Spirit explained it to me. He said that crowns were the people that we helped lead to

Jesus. He told me that I was a Crown for Mrs.___ and that she believed that her death was worth my crown. That she knew that I would be a mouthpiece for Jesus and that I would never stop talking about Him. This finally gave me peace. It still hurts every time I think or speak about it, but I will tell my story to whoever will listen, which is why I am writing this book.

So in July 2005, I was given a court date of August 1^{st,} 2005. Mr. ___'s lawyer had been getting continuances for the past 2 years, trying to get evidence to prove the 2nd Degree- Murder charge. I had been talking to John, my lawyer, on the phone during this time and then met with him the day before the trial to discuss whether or not to be put on the stand. Of course, I wanted to testify, but everyone else was against it. You see, I couldn't just answer a question. I would give way too much information, thinking that I was helping, and they knew that my mouth would get me convicted. But, again, I'm just being honest. So I listened to them, and I prayed and asked God. So I did not testify, which was very hard for me because it was an accident, but no one wanted to believe that.

On August 2nd the trial started. It was during the testimony of Mr.___, that I was finally able to piece it all together. Up until my trial, I did not and could not believe that I had come into contact with anything or anyone other than the guard rails. They had a picture of my van blown up to show the jury. The mark on my van that they were concentrating on was a small round mark behind the right rear tire well. This, they said, was a kickstand mark from Mr.___'s motorcycle. I had never seen that because they confiscated my van on the day of my accident. That's when Mr.___ testified that he was driving behind me and saw me weaving back and forth out of control. He stated that I was at 10:00 to his 6:00. I asked my lawyer what that meant, and he said that this was how policemen describe car accidents and placement. He said that, as described by a clock that, I was ahead of him and to the left. What I and my lawyer and the jury were able to piece together was that when I collided with the guard rail to my left, that I started tipping over on the right 2 tires, and that was when he collided with me. Apparently, he could not slow down in time, and he collided with me while I was starting to roll. My van was out of control, and I never saw him. I thought that when I started to tip over that my van scooted across 3 lanes of traffic and hit the guard rail on the right side of the road, and the impact to my right side was so hard that I started to tip over on my left two wheels. Still, I finally tipped to the right and to the left until I finally ended up on all four tires again. The mark that his lawyer was pointing out was the kickstand on his motorcycle. This was behind my right rear tire well. There is no way from that position or any position that a motorcycle could have impacted my van enough to almost tip me over to the left while already being tipped over on two wheels on the right. And this was why I thought that I had hit a guard rail.

After some time, I went to see the guard rail that had tipped me back over and found no guard rail on the right. I was shocked and amazed. This is why I believe that angels knocked me back over. I truly believed that this was an accident, but Mr.___ could not come to grips with this. I believe that he saw me out of control but could not slow down in time to avoid contact with me. Because of this and the loss of his wife, a great anger and bitterness overcame him. For this, I say again that I am eternally sorry.

For 4 days, evidence was given for the jury to make a decision. These were agonizing and painful days; because I was reliving the accident, and so was Mr.___. I wanted so desperately to say how sorry I was to try to help ease the pain that he and his family were experiencing but could not speak to them. He had many witnesses who tried to paint me in the worst light. It seemed uneven and unfair, and I only had John, my lawyer, and my Toyota mechanic expert; but I had God on my side, and they could not prove that I was driving without brakes; because it was not true. I had brakes!

The jury deliberated for approximately 4 hours and found me not guilty of the Second-Degree Murder charge but instead charged me with involuntary manslaughter. I was found guilty of assault with a deadly weapon with malicious intent to cause harm, felony hit and run, and driving with a revoked license which came up to 47-67months. Because they ran them consecutively, this added up to 4-6yrs in the State Prison that was in Raleigh, NC. I was stunned because this was more than God had told me while living in the barn, but I also had a surreal peace about it. Then Mr.___ and his family got to stand up and tell me how I had affected their lives. They spoke of the pain of losing a wife, a mother, and a grandmother. They looked me straight in the eyes with looks of pain and hatred. I can't even begin to put into words how it made me feel other than extreme sorrow and regret. If I could have traded places with Mrs.___, I would have; but this was not God's plan.

After the criminal sentencing, the judge then stated that I was going to be sued civilly for five million dollars. One of the daughters spoke up and said with eyes full of fury and hate that this would be 1 million dollars for every grandchild that lost their grandmother. I was stunned, not by the amount but by the malice that was directed at me. I so wanted them to understand that it was truly an accident. I looked to my lawyer and asked if I could speak, and he asked the judge, and I was then allowed to address the family. I looked toward Mr. ___ and his family, and with heartfelt words, I apologized. Tears were pouring down my face as they are right now. I told them how very sorry that I was, but they weren't ready to hear it.

After this, I was told that I could say goodbye to my husband, mother, and brother. By this time, I was able to gain control of my emotions, and I gave my rings to my husband and my necklace to my mom. Tommy was being strong for me and was able to keep his emotions under control, but my mother and brother were totally messed up. I hugged each of them and told them how much I loved them; and that I was going to be okay. Then the officer had me turn around as she handcuffed me. This about broke me. This was really happening, and I was now afraid, but I had to be strong for my family. Once we left the courtroom, we walked down a very long tunnel that was under the road that led to the jail. During this time, I started crying and asked the officers what would happen next. They had no sympathy and just told me to be quiet. I realized that this would be the beginning of a new world, one that I wouldn't like.

Once we made it to the jail, I was placed in an orange jumpsuit and placed in a community-style jail. You want to talk about TOTAL CHAOS!!!!! There were so many women talking, arguing, and laughing all at the same time. The noise was deafening after the silent walk through the tunnel. I was given a blanket and pillow and directed to find an empty place to place my blanket. There were women on bunks and women on the floor. The jail was very overcrowded, and I was directed toward the back near the toilets and sinks. A friendly face made room for me on the floor. I'm sure that the look of fear was all over my face. A couple of women on either side of me were kind and started explaining how things worked. I was totally out of my element and overwhelmed by my circumstances. As I looked around, I saw a black lady patting/hitting her head. I thought that she was crazy, and I discreetly pointed at the black lady hitting her head and asked what was wrong with her. I guess the look on my face must have made them laugh, and one of the ladies told me that the lady wasn't crazy-she had just gotten her hair braided, and that was how she scratched her head when it itched. I thought this was very strange, but it was just the beginning of many strange new things.

I can't remember how many days that I had to wait until I went to the State Prison in Raleigh, NC, but it seemed like forever. One day the Enemy was really working on me by telling me lie after lie, causing fear to rise up. In the past, I was able to overcome this by talking out loud to God; but I was afraid to do this here because the Enemy kept telling me that the women would think that I was crazy and then they would put me back in a cell by myself like they did right after the accident. I would rather be in the chaos than be locked up by myself. The women were a distraction, but being by myself unleashed my own inner demons. I could fight the other women, but I couldn't defeat the enemy's voice by myself. I just wasn't strong enough yet. So I started talking to God in my head about my need to talk to Him out loud. That's when the Holy Spirit pointed out the pay phone in the corner. He said that I could pretend to call someone, and then I could talk out loud to God all I wanted to. The noise level was so loud that no one could hear what I was saying; so I walked right over to the pay phone and pretended to make a phone call; and then I started telling God about all my fears and worries, and He listened, and the Enemy left, and I got my peace. Pretty cool huh? I bet that was the first time God ever got a call on a pay phone.

Many women were in jail for just short periods of time, some just doing weekend jail. Whereas others like me were waiting to go to Raleigh. That was where the prison was located. During this time, the women educated me on prison life and what to expect. I couldn't comprehend it, but I was ready to move on to the next part of my journey with God, and my day finally came.

I AM A NEW CREATION

CHAPTER FOUR

As I road into Raleigh North Carolina State Prison for women on the prison bus, I was apprehensive and fearful of the unknown. The ride from Greensboro to Raleigh was an eye-opening experience in itself. We picked up several women along the way from different jails, and for many of them, this was not their first rodeo. Many were hardened and rough speaking. They made me very anxious. They were cussing and smoking- even though the bus driver informed us that smoking was not allowed. They seemed to be tough with their tattoos and short hair. I didn't know what to think, so I kept my mouth shut. Many scary thoughts were going through my head. Everyone has watched one prison show or movie with all the horrors and mistreatments. Fear of the unknown is probably the enemy's second greatest weapon and the first one used. Pride is the number 1 weapon, and pride will normally win out if all else fails. But the Word says in 2nd Timothy, "We are not to have a spirit of fear but of power and love and a sound mind." (right choices and judgments based on the Word of God) I was still young in my walk with God and had a lot to learn. My two years before this were for helping me get my roots deep enough for this day. I would not be uprooted by some women trying to act tough scare me! I would not be uprooted by this storm.

The best part of arriving in Raleigh was that I would finally get to smoke a cigarette. All this anxiety and the smell of cigarette smoke had me craving a cigarette to the point that I thought I could even eat one, but I still had to wait. Once we got off the bus, we had to shower and be body cavity searched. I was appalled. There was no curtain on the shower cubicle, and they just handed me this tiny rough towel and some clothing. When they wanted to do the body cavity search, I didn't know what they were talking about, and one of the girls I had talked to on the way up explained it to me. I was so embarrassed. Once I got dressed in the prison uniform consisting of a light blue short-sleeve shirt and blue jeans with an elastic waistband, white socks, tennis shoes, and a generic bra and panties;

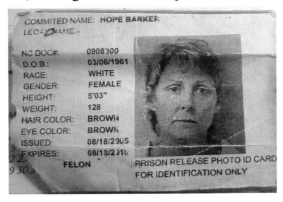

I had to wait in line for my prison picture and ID #. I will never forget mine. It was 0908300. For everything that we did, we had to wait in line. Finally we were ready for the next part of the process, which was to go to the infirmary. Still, someone pulled out a cigarette and lighter and shared a few drags with me on the way. This was the first time I had pulled on a cigarette, and I smoked it so fast that I got lightheaded and sick to my stomach all at once. We then walked single file to the infirmary, where my first experience of prison indoctrination occurred.

The guards/officers love to intimidate new inmates and put them in their place. I call them God's pride killers. As a southerner, I gently touched a person's arm to get their attention, so I walked up to this large male officer to ask a question. As I touched his arm, he jerked away and angrily yelled, "You can't touch me!!!! I can write you up for that." I was dumbfounded and probably looked that way. Still, nature took over, and I apologized, and as I did, I unconsciously touched his arm again. He immediately looked at me like I was crazy, jerked away again, and pulled out a stick like I was going to attack him. It was natural to my nature to touch a person in kindness. This was one of the hardest indoctrinations or institutionalizations. Touch was not allowed by inmates, especially not to officers or anyone that came to prison, other than during visitation. Touch was a write-up offense. As we waited our turn to be seen by the infirmary staff, which took 20hrs, I had many conversations with the people and God. The one I remember the most was, "ok, God, how do You want me to do this? And He said, "I want you to be a hand raising, LORD praising, out loud talking to me kind of Christian." And I said. "Ok."

As my turn to leave the infirmary finally came, and I got to walk down the hill to my new home for the next part of my journey, I raised my hands and praised Him out loud. You see, I knew His voice and trusted Him, and I was going to do like Joyce Meyer's book said. "Do it, afraid." I was afraid of the unknown, but I knew Him.

When you first go to prison, they send you to a separate dorm from the "population" called Reception. They do this to institutionalize you before putting you among the "Lifers, Long-termers, and the rest of the women down the hill. The next phase of God's pride killing/pruning occurs during the month you spend in Reception, and oh, how painful this month is. They want to take away all of your identity and mentally beat you down so that you will be submissive. They blow whistles, yell at you, screaming orders, change rules from one minute to the next, wake you up at all-night hours, and have fire drills. Total insanity! Your pride wants to rebel, but fear takes over, and you learn from others to do what the officers say or get in trouble. You learn to keep your mouth shut and watch and observe. This was not my nature, but my newfound friends helped me out. Until your "canteen is set up, and you get your official ID, you must use what the state supplies. That means no cigarettes. We were separated from the general population, but we would get close enough to them that my friends who had been there before showed me how to beg for cigarettes and when that didn't work, we would surf the ash cans for butts and then smoke them with a lighter that had been thrown to us. Desperate times take desperate measures when you have a cigarette addiction. After your month is up, you finally are assigned to a dorm in "population." Before this assignment, many horror stories are told, which only increases your fear of finally being in prison. Most were lies, but the enemy always tries to paralyze with fear.

My dorm was named Falcon, consisting of four cellblocks with approximately seventy women bunked up in each block (A-B-C-D). I was in the C dorm. You are given a bedroll, a bunk, and a locker. My bunk was at the very back of the dorm, and it was one of the tallest bunks. They had to teach me how to climb up and roll off without disturbing my lower bunkmate. An inmate's space is something that you don't cross. They get really worked up if you touch their stuff or reach over or near their food. The first time I did this, I had no clue that I had done anything wrong, but my bunkmate was quick to enlighten me.

Instead of having a cell, like it is on TV; it's more like the Army. You have approximately seventy women in a space that was designed for about 55 women, and they are all crammed into a small space like sardines in a can. You compete for everything from showers, sinks to brush your teeth, to waiting to use the toilet. By the way, the bathroom toilets are in line with the sinks. There are no doors on the toilets, and while you are taking a dump, another person is brushing their teeth. Every now and then, you will hear someone yell out, "Curtesy Flush!"

You also compete for the blow dryer, curling irons, tables in the day room, fans, and TV time. Being polite is nice but not an attribute that will get you anywhere here. I am describing this so that you will understand there is never a moment of alone time. If you are a professing Christian, know that they will be watching your every move to see if you are real or fake and push your buttons to get a reaction. One thing the "Long Termers(15-25 yrs)" hate is what is called "prison religion." These are people who get religion while in prison to benefit themselves. Once they start to fit in and play the game, and there is always some hustle or another, then Jesus goes right out the door except when it is to their advantage. They talk the talk but don't walk the walk- the same kind of religion that goes on in the world today.

Anyway, they watched me very closely for approximately six months to see if my faith was real or if it was that hated prison religion. The Holy Spirit had instructed me to start my day in the Word by reading two Psalms and one Proverb, and they saw me doing this every morning. I had been reading the New Testament over and over and finally, in 2005, the Holy Spirit instructed me to start at the beginning. I also read books by Joyce Meyer, Max Lucado, Ted Dekker, Francine Rivers, and many others. I didn't cuss and prayed and talked out loud to God. I grew and grew, but I was far from perfect.

I had a quick temper, and I made many mistakes, but the Holy Spirit would have me apologize quickly when I acted in a bad manner. The "Long-termers" began to respect me, and protection came with respect. They had my back and would come to me with prayer requests and questions about God and the Bible. The enemy also came at me through the officers. Don't ever call them a guard. This was a huge offense, which I learned very quickly. The darkness in most of them did not like the light in me; and they would yell at me for no reason other than to yell. Most were bullies, and I learned when not to speak up. I started writing scriptures on a piece of paper, memory verses that were short and sweet, and I placed them in the bathroom. The first stall had a door on it, and I would tape them on the inside of the door. I wrote seven a month, and when you sat down, you could read them and meditate on them. If the officers had known about the Scripture inside the stall, they would have removed it immediately. Funny thing, the inmates never told on me. They actually enjoyed them and would remind me to change them if I forgot to change them each month. Still makes me smile☺

God also told me to start a Bible study. I started teaching the Bible study written by my best friend Teresa Mozena's friend – Katie Souza's, The Captivity series- The Key to Your Expected End. She had written it while she was in federal prison. She actually had a show on Daystar once she got out. Small world, isn't it? It was a Spirit-led study written just for inmates. We needed encouragement. Prison can be very discouraging and for every 10 officers, only one was filled with the light. The rest were led by darkness. Hopelessness was prevalent, and despair takes over without hope. I know that feeling too well. My time before prison, before getting saved, was full of despair. I was bereft without hope. But God knew what it would take to get me to the end of myself. I guess the devil thought it was amusing to take a person named Hope and turn them into despair. It took a car accident and prison to bring hope back to me. Isn't it amazing that I was in prison when my hope came back?

After two years, I finally made it to misdemeanor green. You see, in prison, shirt colors determine the inmate's levels. Tan was for reception-new inmates. Felony blue was for felonies and long-termers, and misdemeanor green was for short-term stays or for those who used to be in blue but finally got their greens which meant they would be ready for transfer to a misdemeanor camp. Misdemeanor green was what everyone wanted, but if you got write-ups, you delayed your ability to get your greens. I remember when I had to go off the compound to see an ENT specialist. I had to be handcuffed and leg shackled to go because I was in felony blue.

I'll never forget how this little girl looked at me and pointed. It was the first time that I had left the prison. I had two guards with me, and I felt very ashamed. I tried to smile at her, but it was hard. I wanted to say, hey sweetie, I'm not a horrible person, but I said nothing. What could I say? But God showed Himself through the officers. They could see how I was affected by being out in public cuffed and shackled, and they were kind and patted me on the back. You can see how easily it was to lose hope and sink into despair. There is a song by Mary Mary, called Shackles. When I hear that song, I remember the physical ones. The next time I had to see a doctor off the compound, I was in misdemeanor green, and it was much better. Green is an encouragement in itself, as a rite of passage. Some women in prison will never wear green.

Now the above shackles were physical ones, but there are invisible shackles that are much worse than the physical ones. A lot of the women that would always wear the felony blue had them, but many people on the outside also have them, and I thank God for removing both.

Now I have to back up a moment. In the spring of 2006, I was getting close to getting my greens. Now, remember, I was still a very immature baby Christian who had a lot to learn and needed a lot of flesh killing to occur. I was 45 years old and a very late bloomer. I asked God to miracle grow me just like a flower, and I think God liked my analogy. Anyway, I believe that I was growing through mistakes and tough times. Here is just one example. Before coming up for my greens, I was caught smoking in the bathroom. We were not allowed to smoke in the dorm.

Now the way it was supposed to work was that they had to catch you with the evidence. I had managed to flush it before the officer came in, but she lied and said she had seen me with a lit cigarette. Now here is the funny part, I was mad because she had lied and written me up while I had lied about not smoking. Go figure! There was definitely something wrong with my logic. I was offended. How could she do this to me? You see, instead of looking inward, I was still looking outward. This was my state of mind. When I read Proverbs, I would think: this was for so and so, or I can use this if someone does this to me. The two-edged sword was fighting outward, not inward, until one day God said," Hope, Proverbs are not for other people; I wrote them to work on you!" What a revelation! I have been such a selfish, conceited person. That is what Galatians 2:20 is all about- flesh killing.

Back to the write-up, I was scared to death. I'd never been to segregation/lockup. It's a jail in a jail. Isn't that funny?! You go before a judge, a prison official who judges write-ups, and you're either pleading guilty or not guilty or guilty with an explanation, basically pleading not guilty. If you plead this way and are found guilty, you get only regular punishment. But if you plead not guilty and are found guilty—you are then given double punishment. I didn't know what to do, so I asked several people who had had write-ups before. They all said to plead guilty with an explanation—but I didn't know what my explanation could be other than, to tell the truth, and I was afraid to do that. I finally asked God what to do the day before my hearing, and I asked him how I should plead, and He said, "What do you think, Hope?" I said, not guilty. You see, my own lies had deceived me. And He said, "Then plead not guilty," which is what I did. I boldfaced lied to the judge. Here I was, a proclaimed Christian believing that it was ok to lie. I believed that God would intervene and that I would be found not guilty. Well, the judge found me guilty, and instead of 15 days in segregation- I got 30. Instead of one month on a $10.00 draw (I'll explain later), I got 2 months on a $10.00 draw, and my greens were shot.

I was so self-centered that I didn't understand why God let it happen this way. So, I went to segregation in another correctional facility- yet different. Unlike Raleigh, which was set up with barracks and open grounds, it was set up like a men's prison with cells and cellblocks and was called Troy. This was a time of reflection and loneliness. To be in a cell all by myself was very hard, but not only was I by myself, but the Lord was also silent. I didn't get any Holy Spirit "Hugs" I truly felt alone. God was testing me to see how I would react. Would I curse Him or keep seeking Him, even when I could not feel Him? I chose to question and then seek Him. I cried a lot, but I kept reading the Word. I kept praying and praising Him. Finally, about day 22, I heard from Him. It was during this time that He told me to write this book.

Of course, I immediately argued with Him. As I write this, I just laugh at my humanity. I argued that writing was NOT my strong suit. I told Him that I was a speaker, not a writer. He continued to inform me that He wanted me to write a book. After many questions and one-sided arguments, I started writing down the weapons that He had given me which will be another book called "War Chest" if God so leads.

Also, He told me that He wanted me to start tithing during this time. I didn't know what tithing was, other than giving money to a church or an organization like Joyce Meyer. Once again, I argued with Him and questioned Him on how I was supposed to do it since I was in prison and did not have access to cash or checks. The only access to funds in prison was the barcode on my ID, and I only got $40.00 per week. He informed me that He wanted me to give 10% of my $40.00 draw to whomever He designated. So, I asked Him what I was supposed to give, and He said He would let me know. Then my flesh woke up and immediately thought about itself and asked, "But God, you know that I'll be on a $10.00 per week draw for the next 30 days." Now let me explain how you draw money. An individual can draw up to $40.00 per week. This rolls over every Monday. If you have family who can send money, then the most you are allowed per week is $40.00. Those who do not have a family that can afford $40.00 can work for 0.40ct-0.60ct-$1.00 per day depending on their job; and then they hustle for the rest. The canteen is where you spend this money on drinks, smokes, candy, makeup, deodorant, shampoo, laundry detergent, stamps, sandwiches, cakes, and so on. When you go to segregation and get punished with a $10.00 draw—then that's all you are allowed to spend, even if you have $40.00. It's very hard to get by on $10.00 / week. My selfish flesh was already thinking about what it would have to give up, so I asked God if I could wait on tithing until after my $10.00 draw was up. Of course, He said no. He wanted me to start while I was still in segregation the next day. That opened up a new set of arguments, but I only received silence.

The next day I decided that I must have heard Him wrong. I just didn't want to do it while in segregation or while I was on a $10.00 draw. You know how that flesh can be, but God knew my heart and had a backup plan. Now I need to explain how segregation was in Troy. For 30 minutes a day, you are allowed to go outside. You walk out single file and get to go into a fenced-in area with a basketball goal, but mostly, you just walk around or talk to each other. During these times, I met a girl in the cell right beside me, and we talked about life and God. I also was given the job of mopping the cell block in the evenings. I enjoyed it because it allowed me out of my cell, and I could quietly talk to the different women and to the one who was in the cell beside me. I would pass notes while I mopped, but you had to do it in a way that did not look like you were doing it.

Anyway, I am explaining this because this was how God would not allow my disobedience in tithing. That Monday, on our 30-minute outing, she said she needed to buy 2 stamps and some soap but didn't have any money or any way to get them. Of course, I knew that this was God's way of saying, "This is how I want you to tithe." I placed my order from the canteen for 2 stamps and a bar of soap and never felt better. It was better to give than to receive.

One more amazing thing happened during this first time in segregation. God delivered me of all my addictions, the final addiction being nicotine, on May 18th, 2006. Hallelujah!! You see, Joyce Meyer taught me about the power of speaking things forth in her book "Me and My Big Mouth." I learned to speak life and not death over myself-Proverbs 18:21. I had been saying aloud, "Lord, I thank you for delivering me of all my addictions." I had spoken it forth every time a desire for alcohol, crack, or whatever had been calling my name. I would say, "I rebuke you, Satan, in the name of Jesus, I've been delivered of all addictions. Thank you, Lord, for delivering me." I spoke that forth for 3 years, and my harvest finally happened during this time of segregation. Things could have gone so differently had I cursed Him instead of praising Him through this tough time. The prison was such a blessing to me; I know that this sounds crazy, but God taught me so many things while there. Another cool thing I learned while in Raleigh was the power of prayer.

There was a sergeant, whose name I won't mention, who was the sergeant of Falcon the dorm where I was housed. She had a photographic memory, and she zeroed in on me. I felt that she was the "spawn from hell," I called her that to others in my early walk in ignorance. This was un-Christian, but I was still a "babe in Christ." I called her this because it seemed like she had it out for me. She would yell loudly, screechingly, and shrilly: "Hope Barker, what are you doing"!!!!!

It didn't matter what I was doing. It would be wrong in her eyes. She closed the canteen window down in my face at least 3 different times—just because she could, and when asked why she would just smirk and smile.

During my stay, I was led to start a bible study, and we would end by standing in a circle, holding hands, and praying. If she could see me outside her window, she would come running out the door yelling, "Hope Barker!! You better stop that right now!!!" We would run and scatter. I didn't understand this because we weren't bothering anyone. Another officer called me aside one day and showed me in the rule book that holding hands in prayer with more than one person was the potential to incite a riot. Crazy huh????? Now you could line/dirty dance with 10-20 women, but holding hands and praying was an offense. Now you know why I thought that she was the spawn from hell.

Anyway, I used to tell God what He needed to do with her, how He needed to do it, and why He needed to do it. I'll never forget the time I had had all I could take. Our dorm quads were set up like a square with the officer's desk in an open area in the middle. The blow dryers and curling irons were kept at the officer's desk because people would hide them in their locker. Many were found when they would do bunk and locker checks. So to get the blow dryer, you had to stand at the door of your quad and yell "Recognize." You were not allowed to exit your quad without permission unless the grounds were open. That occurred 3 times a day for a certain amount of time, but when they were closed, you had to get permission from the officer to step out of your quad. Anyway, I had taken a shower and wanted to use the blow dryer. On this day, the sergeant I won't name was standing at the desk with 2 other officers talking. I went to the door and said: "recognize." She ignored me and kept talking to the officers. I waited politely to let their conversation pause, and when it did, I said, "recognize." She started talking again and ignored me. I waited for another pause and then more loudly said, "recognize," She continued to ignore me. The officers looked at me and then at her, and she started talking again. Well, this flesh of mine had much taming to do, so I lost my patience. I had tried to do this politely and had gotten nowhere, so I yelled recognize more loudly, and again I was ignored. By this point, I had lost any ability to be polite, so I yelled, "RECOGNIZE!!!!!!!!!!!!" She looked straight into my eyes like I was a bothersome little fly; and said, "what do you want, Hope Barker?" I then exited the quad and walked to the desk, and told her that I just needed the blow dryer. She then said, "Why didn't you just say that, to begin with, you didn't have to scream." I just looked at her like she had lost her mind. I was just trying to do things the right way. If I had not waited to be recognized, they could have written me up and I told her so. She looked down at me condescendingly and started making fun of me, and laughed with her officers while I still waited for the blow dryer. I was standing toe to toe with her, but she was about 6 inches taller than me and doubled my weight. I just lost it, pointed my finger up in her face, and yelled, "I rebuke you, Satan, in the name of Jesus!!! You will not steal my peace and joy today!!" I took the blow dryer out of her hand and walked back into my quad. I was not calling her Satan, but I had to rebuke him loudly because he was about to get into my mouth, and I would have said things that I used to before I got saved.

Don't you know that when I got into my dorm, I was telling God what He needed to do with her; and how He had to do it right now!!!! As I was yelling this to God, He clearly and firmly stated, "Hope, I've got her. We need to work on you." I was stunned and speechless, and I asked Him what He meant. He said, "Hope, every time she is mean to you, and you want to tell me what I need to do with her, I want you instead, ask me to change your heart. I want you to ask me to help you love her amid her nastiness, and I want you to pray nice things for her-like peace and joy." I was dumbfounded and amazed, but I wanted to be obedient, so whenever she was mean or nasty, I would do just as He said and pray what He asked me to. Sometimes, it took a lot of prompting from the Holy Spirit, but I eventually got to where I would do it easily. It got to where no matter what she did, it didn't upset me. Instead, amazing love for her would come over me. I know that this sounds crazy, but it happened. I can't describe the genuine smile that would come to my face when I thought about her. Now, this did not happen overnight. It took about 6 months for the transformation in me. Prayer is amazing. Prayer changed me; then God wanted me to take action. (Faith without works is dead)

One day, while doing the laundry, my quad job at the time, He asked me to walk down the sergeant's hall and tell the sergeant, whose name I will not mention, that I loved her. I got an incredulous look on my face and said, "You've got to be joking, God!" He said, "No, I'm not! I want you to walk down that hall and tell her you to love her!" Immediately I started coming up with excuses: it's against the rules to go to the sergeant's office without permission; I could get a write-up; what if she's not there; what if she thinks that I am gay and coming on to her?" God just continued waiting for me to be obedient and tell her. Finally, I said, "Are you sure, God?" And He said, "GO!!!" So, while I was walking toward the sergeant's office, arguing all the way, I got to her door and looked in the window, and there she sat talking on the phone. So, I knocked on the door, and she held a finger up for me to wait. Of course, I was scared that she would yell and write me up, but I waited.

When she finished her phone call, she motioned me to come in; and I took a seat across from her. She looked at me inquiringly, and I quietly and contritely looked down and started telling her how God had put a love in my heart for her that I could not explain; but that I had to be obedient and tell her that I loved her as a sister in Christ; and that I prayed for her. When I looked up, she looked at me with understanding and thanked me. I was surprised, so I quickly got up and left before she changed her mind and remembered I didn't have permission to be there. Obviously, I had the highest permissionGod's permission to be obedient. God's timing is perfect. I found out later that she had been on the phone with her mom, who had had a stroke and eventually died. God always sets us up for success. He knows the perfect time to speak and prepares our hearts to receive. I believe that she needed to hear how much God loved her by using me to tell her and had I not let go of my fear and been obedient, I would never know how amazing prayer could be.

Speaking of obedience, in Raleigh, He taught me the importance of obeying His urgings. By urgings, let me just tell you what He would do. Raleigh was a large compound, much like a big college campus, with dorms, buildings, benches, and many places to walk or sit. I sometimes sat on the ground or bench and watched people go by. By urgings, I mean that I would hear God say, "Hope, I want you to walk up to that girl and hug her and tell her that I love her." He would bring them into my view and expect me to be obedient and do just that. I laugh while I write this; because I remember the first time He ever asked me to do this. I quickly said no and asked him if He was kidding. Thank goodness He understood that I was just a baby and just learning. The first time He had ever urged me to do something I was sitting on a bench across from Master Control, which was where the Warden was. He pointed out a girl in "whites" which meant that she worked in the kitchen. I was just people-watching, and He said, "See that girl there; I want you to walk up to her, hug her and tell her that I love her." I was incredulous, and I just dug my heels in harder and further argued by saying, "But God! What if she thinks that I am crazy, what if she gets mad at me, what if she thinks that I want to be her girlfriend, what if I get a write up—I am across from Master Control you know" He got more stern with His tone and said, "I said to give her a hug, and I mean NOW!" You see, I needed that kind of tone; maybe others don't, but I'm hard-headed and stubborn, and I needed that tone to get me to move.

So, I slowly dragged my feet and started heading toward her. Finally, right before I got to her, I asked God if He was sure about this, and He said that He was. I walked right up to her and obtained eye contact. When I did this, I shyly said, "Excuse me, I'm just being obedient. May I hug you?" She looked at me questioningly, a little stunned, and nodded yes. I then gave her one of those heartfelt, all soul, all body, where the love just flows through you kind of hug. When I started to let go, I looked into her eyes and saw that she had tears flowing down her face. She said, "How did you know?" And I said, "Know what?" and she said, "I was feeling so lonely and desperately needed a hug to let me know that God understood, and you walked up and hugged me."

The biggest smile came over my face-you know, the jaw aching kind and tears started running down my face too; and I said that I didn't know about her conversation with God, but I did know that He loved her very much. I hugged her once more and then walked away, rejoicing and praising Him. I knew one thing after that; I wanted this to happen much more.

It was AWESOME!!! Once again, God's timing was perfect. She was blessed, and so was I. I got to see God at work, and I got to be part of it. Had I not been obedient, I would never have experienced His awesome Glory and to be His Hands and Feet. This is what I live for—what I look forward to each day. Now I would be telling a fib if I said that I was always obedient from that moment forward. It took several more instances with many arguments and stern tones until I finally got it. Now when I get those urges, I get excited.

The prison was also a healing time for me. The Holy Spirit worked with me in so many ways. He helped me deal with my past and accept it for what it was. He then walked me through forgiveness, another weapon in my "spiritual war chest. I will discuss my War Chest in another book if God so leads. Anyway, what I think was the most healing and freeing was when I totally (100%) surrendered to Him. Since I was 6 and was molested, I learned not to trust anyone. Still, when I was drinking or doing drugs, I trusted everyone – especially the wrong people. Sober, I would never totally trust anyone, and the same thing went for God. I still held back a small part of me from God because I didn't want to be hurt or disappointed again. Yet, in the fall of 2005, I 100% surrendered my will to His. There was a fence and razor wire in front of a wall of tall pines, and I would sit in the grass/dirt and look above the razor wire to where the trees and the sky met. This was my "God-spot." I hated razor wire. It represented prison like nothing else could, but I could look up beyond the razor wire to where the green trees met the blue sky, representing freedom. It was where what I wanted didn't matter because I knew that what God wanted was much better. One day I told Him that even if He wanted me to spend the rest of my life in prison, I would do it because His plan for me was so much better than anything I could come up with. I told Him that so be it; I trusted Him totally and that I trusted Him with my life and meant it. This was total surrender—nothing held back. This is a place where everyone must go if they want to be free. That's how God works! It's an oxymoron (surrender=freedom). Crazy, isn't it☺

Once I surrendered, he could work on me; but the enemy also stepped up his pace. By that December, the enemy started attacking me about smoking. Inmates would verbally attack me, saying, "If your body is the temple, then why do you smoke?" I didn't have an answer for that, so several times, I attempted to quit smoking; but my addicted flesh was never able to quit. Finally, I tried once more to quit in my power; and I couldn't even go one hour without taking a puff. I had been smoking a pack and a half for the last 25 years. I had previously tried to quit with

Wellbutrin, hypnosis therapy, and cold turkey, yet failed each time in my power. Let's face it; I was an addict. I wouldn't have been in this mess if I could quit anything on my own. So, one of the last times the enemy wanted to beat me up about still smoking, he said, "What kind of Christian are you? You can't even stop smoking, for God. What good are you? They watch you and see you can't even witness because you smoke. Why bother?" I listened to that voice and started to feel very inadequate believing the enemy; suddenly, the Holy Spirit said, "HOPE! You've never been able to quit anything on your own." He brought to my memory all the times I tried to quit drinking, smoking crack, or taking pain pills. I realized that only God could deliver me and that He would when the timing was right. So, I told the devil that he was right and that I could not quit anything on my own, but God would deliver me; and until that time, I would keep smoking; and he could not make me feel guilty or ashamed about it. It was in God's hands now. I told him he just needed to leave me alone and go somewhere else in Jesus' Name!!

On May 18th, 2006, I heard God say, "Now it's time to quit." You see, I wanted to quit smoking for the right reasons. Not because it was expensive and eating into my canteen money, bad for my health, or I could get written up for smoking in the wrong areas, but because it affected my ability to witness. Of course, it wasn't easy; but the Holy Spirit gave me a scripture to use that helped me to fight the enemy. It was James 4:7. It says, "Submit your works to God; resist the devil, and he will flee from you." Most of us forget the first part and just say the last part, but submitting to God is the most important part!

When the enemy would say, "Just one puff." My job was to fight back by saying, "I rebuke you, Satan, in the Name of Jesus! God has delivered me of all addictions, especially nicotine; now you have to go somewhere else in Jesus' Name." Immediately the thought left. Sometimes he would point someone out who was smoking and say, "Doesn't that look good?" and I would laugh and say no, it doesn't. I would again submit to God by saying, "God, I submit myself to you, I'm resisting the desire to smoke, now devil, you got to go somewhere else in Jesus' Name!!!!! I have been delivered of all addictions since May 18th, 2006. God is GOOOOOOD☺

You see, 1st Corinthians 15:57 says that we already have the victory. Our job is to fight with the Word. With each fight, victory got easier. James 2:17 says that faith without works is dead. I believed by faith that I was delivered. The action required was to fight the impulse with the Word. Now, this is a Word for someone. You see, God explained it to me later. He said that smoking wouldn't send me to hell. He said the most important thing was for me to get to know Him – His Voice, His Word, His love. Then He could and would deliver me of my addictions. He also used my smoking as a way to reach the lost. As I shared my cigarettes, I would witness to others. They also got to see how God can deliver us from addiction. May 18th, 2006 has forever been branded the day My God delivered me of ALL addictions. That in itself is enough to praise Jesus for the rest of my life. Isn't God cool!?

In October 2007, I was finally transferred to Fountain Correctional Center for Women in Rocky Mount, North Carolina; and it was a minimum-security prison. It housed mostly women with 90 days or less; and people like me who had made it to the next level due to time and good behavior. The goal of transferring to a minimum-security compound was to get a job; hopefully off-site, and get a sponsor and eventually get released. Fountain was the next part of my journey and the fine-tuning of my "walk" with God. I still had so much to learn and a lot more pride killing to be worked on. Galatians 2:20 says, "I have been crucified with Christ. It is no longer I who live; but Christ who lives in me; and the life in which I now live in the flesh, I live by faith in the Son of God who loves me and died for me."

What this means to me is that if my flesh is dead, what difference would it make if people call me names or attack me verbally. I'm dead flesh "spiritually," and it shouldn't matter. The old Hope is dead. Do you understand? In theory, this seems simple, but in reality, it's very painful and hard, and I had a lot of flesh-killing to go.

I have three more experiences to tell you about in this chapter. One of my first jobs at Fountain was working in the kitchen, and we cooked for approximately 500 women. You should have seen the huge cooker in which we cooked grits and soup. It was so large that I could have hidden in it. There I had another sergeant, whom I will not name, over the kitchen and staff. One Sunday, I had another flesh-killing event. My cooking partner and I were grilling pancakes for approximately 500 women—that's a lot of pancakes! The huge grill had a gas leak, burning our eyes, making us sick on our stomachs, and giving us headaches. My sergeant was laughing and joking with some inmates in the food line about 10 feet away, and I complained about the gas leak and how it wasn't safe to be cooking. She laughed and thought it was funny, so I said, "You should be over here cooking with this leak, and then you wouldn't be laughing. She then said, "You should shut your damn mouth!"

This shocked me because officers were not allowed to cuss at you, so when I got back to my dorm, I wrote her up for cussing at me on a complaint form and placed it in the slot of a lockbox for that purpose. This was the first time I had done this, but I thought it would be confidential. Well apparently not. Another officer made her aware of the write-up, and she was really after me. At work, she would give me the worst jobs and yell at me and make fun of me, trying her best to get me to respond inappropriately and disrespectfully. She called me a fake Christian, a liar, a thief—anything to get a reaction out of me; but instead, I would sing songs from my Shepherd's Heart bible study group. This made her even angrier. She was doing this because she wanted to be able to write me up and then backdate her write-up and cancel out mine for her, which is what she eventually did. She finally told me to open 3 more cans of green beans in a very nasty tone, and I said, "Yes, Ma'am!" She immediately said, "That's it! That's disrespect. I'm writing you up for disrespecting me!" My jaw dropped open, and I was entirely taken by surprise.

This occurred on December 26th, the day after Christmas. She immediately sent me to the sergeant's office, who in turn told me that I was going to segregation as soon as an officer could get my stuff packed up. Now let me explain how segregation works. As soon as they write you up, they take you to your dorm and have you pack all your stuff up and put it into a bag. That's your clothes, books, and canteen. Some of it goes into storage, and some of it can go with you. Normally, you don't get to take your canteen or your radio when you go to segregation. I had just received my Christmas box full of all kinds of goodies that you can only get once a year. I was upset about it going into storage, but amazingly my canteen and my radio came up with me. Thank you, Jesus. Anyway, she finished helping me finish packing my belongings, and then she asked me to turn around so she could handcuff me. It was cold and raining, and my hands were cuffed behind my back, but she at least placed my raincoat over me since I couldn't. It was just a miserable day. My neck was hurting from an old injury due to the cold and rain, and I just started crying and calling out to God saying, "God, I don't understand this. You know that I didn't do anything wrong. This is unfair, but I am going to trust You anyway. Help me to open my 'spiritual eyes'; so that I may see what you want me to see and learn what you want me to learn. I know that You are going to bless me in this."

Once I arrived at segregation, which was up near administration, they placed me in a cell with another inmate. In my previous experiences in segregation, this being my third time in segregation, I had never had a bunkmate. Isolation was part of the punishment. This time I had a bunkmate, and I started to get excited because I knew God had a plan. Of course, I witnessed to my bunkmate. I answered questions about God and the Bible, and I encouraged her. After six days, I was released from segregation. The sergeant had been mean to other inmates, and they too had started to speak up about it. Because of this, I could go before the Assistant Warden and tell my story. The sergeant who wrote me up was then placed on leave for 30 days while she was under investigation. Finally, after 30 days, she came back from her leave. Due to the write-up she gave me, I had lost my kitchen job and was waiting to be assigned to another job, but I still had to eat in the dining hall where she was still the Sergeant. I was petrified because I knew she had a score to settle with me. She had already been dirty and underhanded in the backdating of her write-up, and I felt very vulnerable. I wouldn't go to the dining hall by myself. I felt that I needed witnesses to help protect me from another crazy write-up. For about two weeks, I was overwhelmed with fear. I spoke forth scripture, such as 2nd Timothy 1:7, "I do not have a spirit of fear, but of power and love and have a sound mind"; and Joshua 1:9, "I am confident and encouraged, not afraid or discouraged, for You are with me where ever I go." I also pled the Blood of Jesus over myself.

Finally, I went out on the "smoke/ ball field where I could get off to myself and started yelling at God. I was crying and yelling and finally yelled, "Lord!!!! You gave me common sense, and common sense tells me not to punch a bear in the nose! Common sense tells me not to run out in front of a Big Mac Truck going 60 miles per hour, and common sense tells me that I cannot trust her!!" I was finally totally spent. I had nothing left. I fell down on my knees and was finally silent. Once I stopped crying and sniffling, I heard God say, "Hope, I'm not asking you to trust her; I'm just asking you to trust Me." When He said that, I finally got my peace, and the fear went away. Isn't it amazing how God works? I never had any more trouble out of that Sergeant. God eventually asked me to apologize to her and ask her to forgive me. It didn't matter who was right or wrong. We are just called to love one another. We were fine after that. Even more amazing was that while in segregation, I learned about my authority as a believer. In segregation, an officer brought me a Kenneth Copeland magazine, and in it was an article on our authority as a believer. We have power and authority over the enemy and his demons. An example that I can give is: that the officers that were not Christians used to give me a hard time. They would change the rules on me and harass me. They seemed nice to the inmates who did wrong but harassed me, and I just could not understand this until one day, I asked God why and He said," because the darkness in them does not like the Light in you." This made sense. I still did not like it, but I now understood why. So, one morning, at their shift change, I noticed that the oncoming officer was one of the mean ones. I quietly (because demons can hear really well) stated, "I rebuke you in the Name of Jesus. I have power and authority over you, and you must be bound or go somewhere else in the Name of Jesus". I then forgot about it and went to breakfast. The next time I returned to my dorm, I noticed that the officer was no longer there and had been switched out with a better one. It totally amazed me!!! I got to see how my authority in Jesus truly worked. It continues to work in amazing ways. I would not have discovered this weapon if I had not gotten that write-up. It was worth every tear and inconvenience.

The next lesson and write-up did not send me to segregation, but it sure pruned off some more flesh. I had finally made it to Level 2. Once you get to Level 2, you can get a job off the compound. Examples of jobs include picking up trash on the highways, mowing and weed-eating grass, or cleaning Government offices. I was assigned to the courthouse. We wore whites with black steel-toe boots. My job was in Wilson, which was 30 minutes away. We rode in a white prison van with no bars on the windows like a normal person. It was wonderful to get to look out and see something other than the prison compound and razor wire. There were automated signs on billboards and they, like moved! We saw restaurants and other people. It was just nice to feel like it was normal again. It was a basic cleaning job and I got paid $1.00 daily to clean floors, toilets, and windows and I loved it. God showed me that there were good judges, DAs, and policemen because they were nice to me and spoke to me like you would a normal human being. This was new since all my other jobs were on the compound with officers in charge.

We were the Wilson workers, and we got up at 5 am and went to the dining hall first so that we could leave for our jobs. The night officer was nick-named "Bad Wig___" because her wigs were always on her head sideways and very unkempt. I think she had a mental illness and the darkness in her did not like the light in me. She was in Raleigh when I was 1st incarcerated and gave me my 1st write-up. She did a locker check and found that I had brought a yeast role back from the dining hall and had it in my locker. You are not allowed to do this because some people make "hooch" with the yeast in rolls and fruit. Anyway, she used to yell at me and call me by my full name, "Hope Barker," trying to get a rise out of me. If I were to react, she could write me up for insubordination. When she found the roll, she said, "What do you think about this Hope Barker" with a very nasty and mean attitude. I was too scared to answer. It was my 1st write-up, and I didn't know what would happen to me. It was dismissed later, but I was too green and new to know how she was targeting me. So, we already had a history when she was transferred to the Rocky Mount Minimum facility. So on this morning, I went to the other side of the dorm to get hot water for my coffee. I had my headphones in my ears listening to HIS radio (a Christian radio station), not paying attention when I looked up, and there she was. She started asking me what I was doing, and I pointed to my cup and said, "getting hot water." She yelled, "Don't you get smart with me, Hope Barker! Let's get this straight.

I'm the officer in charge, and you are the inmate!! You got that?!" I nodded my head and looked at the inmate beside me like, what's up with her?

When the Day officer arrived at 6 am, I was art my bunk. "Bad Wig" ___ started giving her a report. Then she got loud and yelled that the oncoming officer needed to watch me because I had an attitude and that she was thinking of writing me up. Well, my flesh wasn't dead—I should have kept my mouth shut, but instead, I said," All I was doing was getting hot water for my coffee. That's when she yelled, "That's it!!!! I'm writing you up for disrupting pass on." I finally realized that I just needed to shut my mouth. The Word says, "He who guards his mouth and tongue keeps his soul from trouble." Well, I finally did what I should have done to begin with, but I'm still in this old clay body. I sat on my bunk and waited for them to call the Wilson workers to breakfast. Once they called for us to go to breakfast, I was the 1st one out the door. Apparently, she came out and shut the door behind her, not letting any of the other Wilson workers out. As I walked toward the dining hall, she yelled at me, "Hope Barker, I'm writing you up! You need to get this straight—I'm the officer, and you are the inmate! What's my name as she beat on her chest?" I almost said Bad Wig ___, but I caught myself and said, "Officer ___." She again beat on her chest and said, "That's right, and I'm writing you up, so tell me, how do you feel about that?"

Suddenly, I realized that it was just her and me, and I felt very uncomfortable, so I started to go back to the dorm to go back to where the other people were. I went to reach for the door, but she took her umbrella, poked it toward me, and blocked the door with her body. I told her that I wanted to return to the dorm, and she said "no!" and poked her umbrella at me, and I could tell that something wasn't really "RIGHT" with her, like she was unhinged. That's when I noticed the inmates looking out the windows, watching. I started yelling, "Help, Help, someone let me in!" You could see that someone was trying to open the door, but she was holding it closed with her body (she was a very large woman). I again yelled, "Help, Help! Open the door!!" Finally, she came to her senses and stepped away from the door. The officer on the other side of the door came flying out since there was no longer any resistance. Then Bad Wig ___ calmly says, "Hope Barker, why are you out here?" I was speechless. I ran past her into the dorm, shaking, and went to my bunk. They called for the Wilson workers a 2nd time and finally let us all go to the dining hall. Once we were finished with breakfast, the

Wilson workers were called to go to work. While on my way to the van, they stopped me and said I could not go off the compound because I was under investigation. I was stunned. Not only did I again lose my job, but that weekend was my first time off the compound with my sponsor. She was going to take me out to dinner at the Hibachi Grill. Everyone works hard to do right so that they can get to the next level and the next freedom, but mine got cancelled all because of this crazy officer. I didn't realize at the time that God was working on my control of my mouth, but it didn't make it hurt any less or that it was any less wrong. To me, this was total insanity and made no sense.

So, for 53 days, I waited without a job to see the DOC Judge to plead my case. During these 53 long days, I started "prayer walking" on the smoke/ball field. The inmates would smoke and play cards and gamble at the picnic tables. I would be walking and praying out loud, and they would watch. Some of them would encourage me about the write-up—even those who weren't living for God were watching to see how I would act.

You see, sometimes things happen so others can see how a Christian handles it. Do they revert to worldly ways, or do they keep their faith and trust in God? I believe that God was allowing me to be tested and to let others see how I reacted. After watching me, even the unbelievers were cheering me on. At the end of 53 days, I finally went before the DOC, and they dropped the charge. They said it had passed the specified time limit so that I could not be found guilty. This was their way of saving face. Still, my next level had been placed on hold, and it was a hard pill to swallow. Again, I just had to trust God. Everyone celebrated my victory and was able to see that I had passed God's test and theirs too. By this time, I had started working in the canteen and loved this job. It was the best one so far, but God had a different plan. The administration said that Wilson wanted me back. I didn't want to go back. I liked what I was doing, and now I had to return to Wilson and lose my canteen job. So here goes my flesh again, I was irritated and frustrated, and I went back to the smoke/ball field to yell at God. I got away from everyone else and started yelling, "I just don't understand this, God!! It's just not fair!! Every time I get a job I like, it gets taken away from me. Is this how it is always going to be? It's just not fair!!!!" I just started "ugly" crying and then finally got quiet. God said, "Did you not tell me that I could use you however and wherever I needed?" Then I got a picture in my head of all 4 of Paul's journeys (he is my Bible person idle). Immediately I felt convicted and ashamed of my attitude and words. I told God how sorry I was and asked Him to forgive me.

I started learning to stop placing my wants first. Our fleshly nature is very self-centered and selfish, and I feel that I am one of the worst, yet God still loves me. After this, He started showing me moments on the compound or in Wilson where He had used me to pray for or encourage someone. You see, it's not ALL about us. I truly started to try to live what I was talking about. Surrender.

I have shared many examples of hard times but also many amazing times. I met my very 1st true best friend while in Raleigh. Her name was Teresa Richards Mozena. It was the most amazing sisterhood and friendship. Once I moved to Rocky Mount, NC, I joined the choir. The Chaplains were Mr. & Mrs. Coley, who was such a blessing to me. I loved singing to the LORD. God also blessed me with new friends and sisters in Christ: Amber, Traci, and Marie. I met wonderful volunteers who taught me that the Christian life could be fun and doable. Beth, Patricia, Carol, Pricilla, and Judy took me into their homes and hearts and lived it in front of me. The devil says that it can't be done- that life will only be boring and horrible and that you will never have friends or fun again. They taught me that this, too, was a lie.

My prison term finally ended, and I was released on July 8th, 2009. My husband picked me up, and as we drove away, I waved with a HUGE smile on my face to those who were still there, looking forward to the next part of my journey.

CHAPTER FIVE

As I previously stated, I was released from prison on July 8th, 2009. Everyone dreams of the day that they get out. This was the day we long for and it had finally come and I couldn't believe it. I had made so many plans in my mind about what the 1st thing that I would do would be. But I also knew that the enemy would be waiting for me when I left the prison gates, so I had asked my mentors and bible study leaders from Shepherd's Heart Bible Study to come and pray for me before I left. Carol and Pricilla came, and we prayed so long that the guard at the gate yelled at us and told me that I had to leave now. We laughed so hard, and I said that I bet that this was the first time the guard had to tell someone that it was time to leave. We hugged and told each other that we would keep in touch, and I hopped in Tommy's car and took off for Martinsville, Virginia, and freedom. It was surreal. As we drove down the road, I had to keep telling myself that this was really real. After we had driven several miles, we passed the exit for Wilson, and I told Tommy about my job there. At times I was a chatterbox, and at other times I was pensive and quiet. This was all so strange and new. It was a 5 hour drive to

Martinsville, and Tommy was so very excited to have me with him, and he started talking about the apartment that he had for us and how he had furnished it. He spoke about the clothes that he and my mom had bought for me and how he had set up a checking account for me. He told me about his job and how he had come over to the apartment to move things in when he would get off from work. He was very proud of the fact that he wanted me to have everything that I would need, and I was so very proud of him. He told me about how he and my mother had become friends and that they met for lunch in Roanoke on several occasions to choose items for the apartment and me. He said this in amazement because they had not tolerated each other prior to my accident.

Now, I need to backtrack. As an alcoholic and addict, one of my coping mechanisms was to pit my mother and husband against one another so that I always came out the winner. My husband despised my mother, and my mother despised my husband. This started early on in our relationship, and I continued to do this until God made me aware of what I was doing while I was in prison. I always wondered why they did not get along, and God explained that I was the cause. Once I understood what I had done, I asked Him to help me to never do it again. This happened while I was in Rocky Mount, North Carolina, in 2008. I then wrote my mother and asked her to start praying for Tommy. I asked her to ask God to change her heart and to help her to love him. I then told her that prayer changed things and told her the story of when God had done the same with me with the Sergeant in Raleigh. When she responded, she said that she just couldn't do it, that there was too much bad blood between them. I called her on the phone and begged her to just please try—that God would help her with the feelings—just to ask God to help her love him regardless. She said, "I don't know, Hope, but I will try." Of course, God changed her heart like He changed mine with the Sergeant. Once her heart changed, then Tommy did too. He was amazed about the change in her and actually said, "I really like Toby and have enjoyed spending time with her." Prayer really does change things and people. Isn't God AMAZING!!!!!

For the rest of the trip, I just sat back and looked out the window, seeing things with the new eyes of freedom, listening to Tommy chatter on with excitement. In my heart, I was thanking Jesus all the way home.

Once we arrived in Martinsville at the apartment, Tommy walked me up to the 2nd floor, and at the end was a swing.

He was very excited and he could hardly contain it. I always loved porch swings, and he reminded me of that and said that we could go and buy some flowers and plants to place out there because he also knew that I loved plants and flowers. His love was so amazing, and his excitement was contagious. He gave me a tour, showing me all the things that he had bought. He showed me the dishes and spoke about how he and Nana had put everything up, down to the shelf paper in the cabinets and the spices. I loved him very much in that moment. Tommy told me that mom had bought us a very expensive mattress and that they had gone to pick it out together. That night I slept the best that I had slept in a very long time.

I got out on a Wednesday and was already planning on going to church on that Sunday. While in prison, Tommy had asked around about churches. He knew the kind that I liked. He had been going to his mother's church, but knew that I was a Pentecostal. There is a big difference between Baptists and Pentecostals, and Tommy had asked around and said that he thought that Mercy Crossing would be just perfect. You have no idea how much this meant to me. This showed me how much he really loved me; by caring enough to search for a church for me. On Sunday, he drove me to Mercy Crossing, and as I walked through the doors and was greeted by the greeter with a big smile and handshake, I knew that I had found a church home. Once the service was over, I met the pastor and his wife, Jackie and Sherry Poe. They welcomed me with open arms, and she gave me a big hug. That sealed it.

For the first few weeks, I just started to settle into a routine. You have to understand that in prison, you make maybe 25 decisions a day. Your choices are very slim, but once you get out in the real world, the decisions seem to be limitless. It can be very overwhelming and stressful. The first night I got home, Tommy and his mother, Nana, and I went to a barbeque restaurant. Once we were seated, they handed us menus, and I became overwhelmed. Too many people, too many choices, and I sort of shut down. Tommy noticed immediately, and I told him that it was culture shock. I asked him what he thought was a good choice for dinner, and he helped me with what to choose. I know that sounds very silly, but after having been in prison for 4 years, it's a big, big change. Gradually I got over that, but it was very overwhelming that 1st day back.

I finally settled into a routine, and the next thing on the agenda was to get my social security card and driver's license. Tommy worked for a local home builder as their lead plumber 12hrs a day, and I was by myself for a long time. I watched a lot of TV and read my Word, but after having been surrounded by women constantly for the last 4years, I was very lonely. I decided to meet my neighbors. The couple on the 1st floor across from me had a dog, and that was my way to get to know them. I love animals and went down to pet the dog, and I introduced myself. I met another lady and her brother because they too had dogs, and I started to feel a little better. That Saturday, Tommy took me to Roanoke, Virginia, where my mom lived. My brother Howie, my sister-in-law Doreen and my nephew Jared, and my niece Olyvia, were there to welcome me home. I cannot describe the joy that I experienced when I hugged my mother and brother. We were a family that was reunited, and that is what God is all about. You see, the devil hates love and family, but my God is Love and the restorer of family.

Once I had my social security card and my driver's license, I started to actively pursue a job. A lot seemed to have changed since I last attempted to get a job. I was used to going to the place of business and speaking to the person hiring and then filling out an application while there. At this time, Martinsville had the highest unemployment rate in the state of Virginia, which was 25%. But I knew that if I could just get my toe in the door to talk to someone, I would get hired. The problem, to my dismay, was that everything was now done online. So, I started applying for jobs online, but there was always a question at the end that asked if I had ever committed a Felony. Well, of course, I had. Also, I was applying everywhere except in healthcare, where all of my experience had been for the last 13 years. In addition, there was a 7-year gap without any employment. No one, I mean NO ONE, wanted to hire me. I received no response from anyone. This was all so very discouraging. Add to that; I was still struggling with my new environment and very lonely. I was still going to church, and I was attending Wednesday bible study, but otherwise, all I did was housework and watch TV and apply for jobs that I knew that no one would hire me for. Depression started setting in. In addition, I was overweight. While in prison, the only pleasure that I got other than going to church and mentoring others was in food. They had these cakes that we called "Fat Girl Cakes." They were honey buns with filling or icing or doughnuts. Also, I would have a snickers at least once a day, plus bubble gum and chips and tons of other fattening things from the canteen. While doing Crack, I had gotten down to 89lbs; and now I weighed 150lbs. My body image was awful, and

I felt ugly once again. My Mom and I talked about it, and I tried cabbage soup, dieting, and exercise but did not lose any weight. My mom had a nice bike that she only rode when they went to the beach, and she offered it to me. I started riding it at 6 am around the neighborhood. I went at 6 am before the humidity and heat made it impossible. I would put on my headphones with my iPod and listen and sing my Christian music. It was wonderful, but one morning a deer almost collided with me. It frightened me badly. I became fearful when riding, and God knew this, so the Holy Spirit said, "Hope, why don't you pray that God give His traveling Angels charge over you to protect you while you ride your bike or drive your car, trusting and believing that the deer will either hit an invisible wall and bounce off of you, or invisibly just go through you without causing you harm. Trust and believe in your prayer." Well, I did pray this prayer, and I trusted and believed in God to protect me with His traveling Angels. I still pray this prior to getting in my car and trust and believe. He's such a good God.

Ok, back to the job search. Finally, one morning, the devil was really beating me up, saying things like, "No one will ever hire you. You have felonies; you have gaps in your work history; you are worthless and unwanted." I started to listen to that voice when the Holy Spirit said, "Hope! God could send someone to your front door and hire you. He's the one who 'owns the cattle on a thousand hills.' He's the giver of jobs. He is YAWEH Yireh, your Provider." This was all of the encouragement that I needed. I yelled at the devil while facing my front door and told him what the Holy Spirit had just told me. I told him that if God wanted me to have a job, then He could walk right up to my front door and give it to me. I told him that he needed to shut up in Jesus' Name and go somewhere else. He immediately left, and peace returned. God's cool like that. I then told God that if I didn't get a job until I got my nursing license back, I would be fine with that, but I needed something to do. I needed to volunteer somewhere or do something because just staying in my apartment was not good for me. I spoke with my mother-in-law, and she said that her church gave canned goods to a local organization and they helped people that were in need. She said that I could go there and possibly volunteer. I called them the next day and went in to fill out the paperwork. It was near the end of October, and they had a place called the "Pumpkin Patch," where they sold pumpkins for fall and Halloween. I went the following Monday with another lady to sell pumpkins and load them in people's cars. God gave us some time with no customers, and of course, I shared my story. You see, "I am not ashamed of who I am today. I am a new creation, old things have passed away, and I am brand new." In fact, I am a princess because my Dad's a King.

Anyway, once I shared my story, a man in a white van pulled up with the local cleaners on the side. He got out of the van, and I walked up to him and asked how many pumpkins he would like. I was smiling and walked around with him, pointing out our best pumpkins. He finally picked out 10 for his 3 stores. I then helped him to load them and took his money. I then started to walk back toward the pumpkins when the other volunteer yelled my name and placed her hands together in a prayer position, and then she pointed to the van. I took that to mean that I should ask the man from the van for a job. He was getting ready to back out when I ran up to his window and knocked on it. He rolled down the window with a questioning look on his face, and I just blurted out, "Do you have a job?" he looked at me like I had 3 heads, and I said, "I need a job. Do you have a job?" he still looked at me like I had lost my mind and said, "You want a job?" and I said, "Yes! I need a job!" He then really looked at me and said, "Well, actually, I have a job opening up right now. Why don't you go to my church street store and fill out an application? Ask for Sue, my manager." I thanked him profusely and then ran over to the other volunteer and burst into laughter. I told her what he said, and I thanked her for the encouragement from God. I was so excited. I could not wait to see Sue. She told me to go ahead and go right then. I asked if she was sure, and she said that she would be fine. I hugged her and hopped into my car, and went straight to the local cleaners. When I got there, I asked for Sue and told her that I had just spoken to Avery Mills and asked for an application. She gave it to me, and I went home to fill out the application. I called the next day and met with Sue and Avery. This was a dry-cleaning business, and he had 3 stores. The actual dry cleaning was done at the Church Street site, but he delivered the clean clothing to the Collinsville and Greensboro road sites via van. I would work from the church street site and pick up the dirty clothing in the mornings and return them cleaned in the afternoons. He said that he had one other applicant and I started to get a little anxious, and then I shared my story with Sue and Avery. They were awesome. They did not judge me. They did not look down on me. They actually smiled at me and were amazed and welcoming. Their only concern was my driving record and how that could affect his insurance. He asked me to go to the DMV and get my driving record so that he could present it to his insurer. I left feeling a little worried. The voice in my head was saying, "Well, that's that. You will never get the job now. In fact, you will never ever get another job. You are worthless and a drag on everyone." But my best friend, the Holy Spirit said, "Hope, this is a God thing. Your God does not get your hopes up just to dash them. He loves you and has great plans for you. Not to harm you but to prosper you and give you hope and a future. Don't listen to his lies."

So, when I pulled into the DMV, I was nervous but excited and hopeful. I filled out the paperwork and handed it in, and then waited rather impatiently. If anyone reading this has been to the DMV, then you know what I mean. Finally, they called my name and handed me a copy of my driving record. I didn't look at it until I got to my car, and then when I opened it, it said that I had zero points. I shouted Hallelujah with my hands in the air and sped back to the local cleaners. Of course, they hired me. It was my 'God job.'

Avery and Sue were wonderful; they supported me and encouraged me, and I enjoyed working again. Work gives me a sense of self-worth and a feeling that I am contributing. It was only minimum wage, but it was something. Once I got my first paycheck, I knew that I had to send a portion for my restitution. I asked God how much should I send to Mr.____ and He said $20.00 monthly. I was not allowed to be in contact with Mr.___ due to my 9 months post-release contract, so I contacted his lawyer that was in Greensboro, North Carolina. I sent him a money order for $20.00 and asked that he forward it to Mr.___. This was in November, and I sent another money order at the beginning of December. On Christmas Eve, I received a letter from Mr.___'s lawyer with my two $20.00 money orders stating that if I could not pay $160,000.00 in one lump sum, he didn't want anything at all. I was blown away. This was my Christmas gift from God. He knew that I would never be able to pay $160,000.00 in a lump sum. This was God's way of saying, enough is enough; you have done your time and do not need to do anything more. You see, while in prison, they sued me civilly for $5,000,000.00-- $1,000,000.00 for every grandchild that lost their grandmother. I was blown away. It truly was just an accident. If I could have died that day instead of her, I would gladly have done so; but I was not the saved person Mrs. ___ was. While in prison, my civil attorney and I met and negotiated the $5,000,000.00 down to $160,000.00. Either way, it was an impossible amount for me. I struggled and struggled with her death. This was an area where the Enemy could really beat me up. Even though it had been an accident, I still felt very responsible, and it was trying to kill my soul. Finally, the Holy Spirit took the Enemy's weapon away. He said, "Hope, Mrs.___ says that you were worth her death. She said that you are a 'Crown' for her." I may have said this before but this is important. You see, before prison, I thought that the Crowns that we lay at Jesus' feet were made of gold and silver, but today I understand that they are symbolic for the people that we lead to the LORD. I was a Crown for her, and the Holy Spirit told me that she said that I was worth it. Do you have any idea what that meant to me? The biggest torture that the enemy used against me was her death, and now she wanted me to know that I was worth it. I hadn't felt worth anything for so long, and then Jesus came into my life because of her. He also said that she said that she knew that I would never be quiet about Jesus or how He came into my life. I still have a hard time even thinking about this, and whenever I do, I can't help but cry and feel sorrow; but then I believe what she said about being worth it. I can't wait to meet her in heaven and give her a big hug. I have prayed for Mr.___ and his family every day and hope that one day they will be able to forgive me. Grace is amazing.

By the springtime, I decided that I wanted to start a pick-up delivery service for Avery. He had been so very kind and supportive of me, and I wanted to pay him back. My Father-In-Law used to say that I could "Sell ice to an Eskimo." I sold jewelry at Jewel Box when it was downtown, and I also had been top sales at the Mazda Dealership before becoming a nurse. So, I started "cold calling" on businesses all over the area from Martinsville, Collinsville, and Bassett. Once I picked up a business, I went on to the next. My pick-up route turned into a 3-hour trip. I would pick up on Mondays and return on Thursdays. When God led, and I had time, I would share my story. He always set me up for success. You see, Mrs.___ was right. I could and would not shut up about what God had done for me. I was no longer ashamed of my past; it was no longer who I was. The old Hope had gone away, and the new Hope was here to stay. Also, during the spring, I started to earnestly pursue getting my nursing license back. I was writing to the Virginia Board of nursing, but they told me to contact the North Carolina Board of nursing. I felt like they were "passing the buck"- me- back and forth. Once I got in touch with the North Carolina Board of nursing, they told me that they would help me to go through the Virginia Board. See what I mean. Anyway, I finally started to make headway, but they said that they could not do anything until my 9 months post-release was complete. This meant that if I violated my 9 months parole, I could go back to prison for 20 more months. My sentence had been 47-67 months, and I had served 47 months. I had to go and check in and see my parole officer and get urine tested every so often. Lisa was my parole officer, and Tim was the Chief. He was also my Sunday school teacher and the leader of Christian Recovery. They both were the best. They supported me and encouraged me. They were my friends, and they were AWESOME examples of how Christians should be. My church, Mercy Crossing, was also amazing. They welcomed me with open arms. Pastor Jackie and Sheree loved me. Once my church family got to know me, they did too. Of course, I shared my story. These were "walk it, talk it Christians," and they asked me to be a Life group leader. I was humbled and excited! I had always wanted to lead a Bible Study. Joyce Meyer, my "spiritual mom," had started out that way, and look where God had taken her. I led a "Women's" group that consisted mostly of women that I had met at AA or Christian Recovery and a few women from my church. You see, God does not allow us to go through hard times just to go through pain. We place ourselves in these situations through "free will." Instead, once He helps us through and changes our hearts, He then wants us to be His hands and feet to help others going through similar situations. Joyce Meyer, Judy, Sandra, Betty, Kim, Julie, Patricia, Beth, Carol, and Joanna were his "Hands and Feet" for me, and God has used me and continues to use me for others. That's what it is all about once you are a Christian. In fact, it's why I look forward to each day.

Anyway, the board told me to call them back when my 9 months were up and to start doing continuing education electives while I waited. My mom had bought us a computer, and I started refreshing my nursing. By May, my 9 months were up. The board doesn't move fast. I sent in all the paperwork and would send them my continuing education certificates as I completed them. I was also starting to be a leader in Christian recovery. I really enjoyed this. You see, almost everyone that was close to me tried to discourage me from seeking my nursing license. They were afraid that I would not get it back and be very disappointed and hurt. The only people that believed in me were my Christian Recovery friends and Lisa, Tim, Avery and Sue. What people didn't understand was that my God does not Dangle a carrot in front of His "Child" and then jerk it away. When my God promises something, then he follows through.

I finally had an appointment set up for February 14th with the Virginia Board of Nursing in Richmond, Virginia. The closer it got to that day, the more the Devil tried to discourage me and cause me to doubt. It was a battle. I fought and fought with the Word, but by January, he was starting to wear me down. Finally, My Papa God said, "My child, I love you. What better day to show you than Valentine's Day; of course, I hand-picked the day. My timing is always perfect. Trust Me." My sense of peace came back and stayed with me right up to the day I went to my brother Howie's house in Partlow, Virginia, and stayed the night. My sister-in-law, Doreen, went with me for support.

Now I have to back up for a minute. Our local hospital was on my pick-up delivery route for Avery. God had given me a desire to work there when I obtained my nursing license. My contact at the hospital was the Director of Human Resources, and her name was Sherry Scholefield. Every time that I drove to the hospital, I would ask God if today was the day to share my story, but I never got the go-ahead until 2 weeks prior to going before the Board. On that day,

I pulled the van into the hospital and asked, "Is today the day, God?" and He said, "Yes!" I started to get excited. I knew that He had something really amazing for me. When I went into the reception area, I asked if Sherry was in and available. Of course, she was in and available!! I went back to her office and hung her clothing on the door hanger, and sat down to chit chat. She smiled at me and asked me if I still liked my job, and I told her yes but that I would not be doing it for much longer. She looked at me questioningly and said, "No?" and I told her that I had been a nurse and then shared my story. Once finished, she asked me if I wanted to work there. I told her, of course, and then told her that I had been a Medical-surgical Telemetry nurse before my accident. She immediately went to her computer to see job availability. She did not have any Med-Surg-Tele positions available but did have a Critical Care position open. I had never done Critical Care and was unsure. She then called the Nursing Director from Critical Care and asked her to come down and speak with me. I gave her a brief synopsis of my story and said that I would be going before the Board to get my license back on February 14th. She explained the Job, and they both offered me a job right then. Wow!!!! Isn't God amazing?! I had a job even before getting my license back. So, on February 14th, I went before a 5-person board panel with my sister-in-law. The Virginia Board of Nursing is the scariest group of people that I have ever encountered. Prison guards had nothing on them. Finally, after multiple questions, they asked me, "If we decide to give you your nursing license back, what would you be most afraid of?" I thought about it long and hard and then smiled with really big tears in my eyes and said," "Not a thing. I would just be so very thankful and blessed to be given a 2nd chance to be a nurse again and do the thing I so dearly love." I then had to step out and wait for what seemed like forever, but of course, I got my license back. I am writing about it, aren't I? He is such a cool God. I have a little side note.

In the Bible, many people had special names for God, like Hagar Sarai's maidservant. When she was cast out to die, God spoke to her, and she called Him "El Roi-The God who sees me," or another name was "YAHWEH Rophe" The God Who Heals me." Ann Spangler has a book, "Praying the Names of God," and in it are several Hebrew names of God and a study. My name for God has been, "The Coolest God Ever", and I always wanted to know how to say it in Hebrew; so, I knew that ever was El Olam, and I googled coolest in Hebrew, and it was Sababa. So, my name for God is "El Sababa Olam- The Coolest God

Ever!!" I just had to say that. You can't say that name without smiling☺

Okay, back to my story. You know, we all have a story. I once heard Kirk Franklin say that we were Living epistles. Isn't that cool? The return of my nursing license had a few stipulations: I had to complete a nursing refresher course since I had been out of nursing for 7 years. I had to be evaluated by a psychologist, and I had to go to 2 recovery meetings a week for a year. I completed an online course through Chapel Hill in 3 months-it was a 6month course; do you think that I was excited? The first psychologist was not a Christian and did not understand my transformation, so I asked a friend in my Church, Diane Taylor, and she suggested Regina Curtis-Davis. She's a Holy Ghost-filled woman of God, and she was perfect. The only thing that frustrated me was that I had to go to 2 recovery meetings. I was already in a leadership role with Christian Recovery; why did I have to go to an AA or NA meeting. I had been delivered of all addictions on May 18th, 2006. Now let me explain. People can attempt to stop their addictions in their own power but are truly never free. The desire is always in the background. I wanted deliverance in God's Power. Joyce Meyer taught me the power of the tongue in her book, "Me and My Big Mouth." While in the barn, I started changing how I spoke. Instead of always speaking negative, self-hate, self-destructive words about myself or things other people had said about me, I started saying what God said about me. At the end of the book, I am going to write the life verses that I say about myself when I get up in the morning. Anyway, I started speaking forth, "Thank you, Lord, for delivering me of ALL addictions.

Especially_____ (fill in the blank) if I was having an urge for alcohol or crack or a cigarette, that's what would fill in the blank. I spoke this forth for 3 years before it finally occurred. In prison, you can still get most anything that you want for the right price. Homemade "hooch" was made with fruit and loaf bread. People smoked crack out of drink cans and chicken bones, and people would also sell their psych meds. The Holy Spirit gave me the "sword" to fight with. It was James 4-7, "Submit your works to God, Resist the Devil, and he will flee from you." Now instead of trying to quit in my own power, I had God's Word (the Sword) and God's power to fight and win. You see, where thoughts go, actions follow. I had to fight the thought with God's word and prevent the action. In the beginning, I was speaking forth this scripture about 4 times an hour, but eventually, it became once an hour and then once a day, and then once a month until I was truly walking out my deliverance. I still occasionally will have a thought or desire for a cigarette or alcohol, but I immediately say my verse, and the thought goes away. God is ABLE!

So, when the Board required me to go to 2 meetings a week, I whined to God. I was fussing and saying, "Why do I have to do this, God? You delivered me of all addictions. Why do I have to do this?" God said, "It's not all about you, Hope." You see, God had people hand-picked for me to encourage and mentor. They were at the meetings. I could not have been his hands and feet if I did not go to them. Jesus came for the sick- not the well. God had delivered me of addictions, and he wanted me to help others. The "Gift" that I am used the most by is Exhortation (to encourage and admonish others in all wisdom).

The sad part is that very few people want deliverance bad enough to do whatever it takes. I had only one success story, and that was Vickie Wooten; but I have to realize that the Word says in Matthew 7:14, "Because strait is the gate, and narrow is the way, which leads to life, and few will find it." Thank God for Vickie and me. You know that Jesus would have gone to the Cross for just one person. That's how much He loves us.

Once my refresher course was completed, I went to the hospital and started working on June 27th, 2011. I started working in the Critical Care Unit and was so very excited. I had never worked in Critical Care and was a little anxious, but I knew that I had the Holy Spirit to help me. Ventilators and Critical Care IV drips were what intimidated me the most, and several times a day, I would go into the bathroom and tell God that I was not capable of doing this and document all that was needed; but I knew that He was able. You see, CCU is a very life-and-death kind of place. One mess-up could be a person's life. There are medications called "pressors" that affect the blood pressure, and if your dose is wrong, they can die. I'll never forget the first time that my preceptor and the respiratory therapist and I transported my first ventilated patient down for a CT Scan. He had multiple IV drips, and the therapist was bagging him as we entered the elevator, just barely fitting in. There was a portable monitor that went with him, and I was constantly looking at his vital signs while also watching the respiratory therapist squeeze the Ambu bag. It all seemed very out of control. I was thinking, what if the blood pressure bottoms out while we are in here. What if he codes on the CT table? I was petrified!! In my mind, I kept saying," please don't let him code, Lord" We made it there and back without any event, but I very quickly came to realize that I was in control of nothing, and God was in control of everything. Once out of orientation, I started saying "Help me, Lord" out loud without even realizing it. I shared my story with everyone that the Holy Spirit led me to. I have my ID picture that I was given when I first went to Raleigh for prison, and I would show it to the people that I shared my story with. They would look at me in astonishment, and I would say, "And those are only the outside changes." Everyone from the CEO and the CNO down treated me with awe and respect. No one ever looked down on me. A large part of that was the favor of God, but also, they could see the awesome transformation of God in me. I would say to them that I was no longer ashamed of my past; the past was not who I was. "I was a new creation. Old things had passed away, and behold; I was brand new."

One area that the enemy could still make me feel shame over was no longer having a house. My husband worked very hard on furnishing our apartment. It was beautiful, but the enemy would show me mind pictures of our house in Greensboro. I loved our house, and I felt security in having a house. The Devil would remind me of all of the stupid things that I had done in order to lose our house because of crack cocaine. I would ride through the neighborhood dreaming about buying a house. But then the devil would remind me of all that I had lost and cause shame yet once again. Finally, I had had enough, and I told God that I would be fine with living in the apartment until I moved into my Heavenly Mansion; but I needed His help to get over the shame of having lost my house. He said, "Hope, I am going to buy you a home, and I am going to pay cash for it!" I was blown away! I believed Him, but then my flesh stepped in. Since He was going to pay cash for it, then I thought that I needed to look at lesser expensive houses to help Him out. Now isn't that crazy? I believed that He would buy me a house, but I thought that I had to help Him since He would be paying cash. I was so excited. I told everybody. Most everyone thought that I was nuts, but I didn't care. I knew that my God was able. I would ride my little red car, a 1991 Mazda Miata that my mom had gotten me while I was still in prison. It had been something for me to look forward to. She loved me so much. She was my champion while I was in prison. She supplied my money for the canteen, and she wrote me always. She used to draw silly stick man pictures of herself to make me smile. I miss her so much.

Anyway, for the next 6 months, I would drive through the neighborhood looking at houses, envisioning us living in one of them. Mulberry road and the Forest Park area were always my favorite homes. Mulberry road was the most beautiful road with gorgeous old trees that hung over the road. It looked like a Fairytale in springtime. At the end of Mulberry road was a Country Club and I envied the kids that belonged there when I was in high school. They used to have the best dances and parties there. Anyway, after about 6 months, God said, "Hope! My name is NOT the God of Settles!!! My name is El Shadday, Almighty God!! Don't you be settling for less! Don't you understand that I have an awesome and amazing house picked out just for you?" I was shocked and amazed. I realized that I did not need to settle for anything. So, after that, I would drive through the neighborhood looking at any and all houses with excited expectation—just waiting for His perfect home for us. One Sunday, Tommy and Nana, and I were driving through the neighborhood looking at homes for sale, and we saw this one that had a brand new for sale sign in the yard. It was very nice, and Tommy and Nana thought that this was the one. When we got home, Tommy was so very excited. We talked, and he asked me to call the bank and the realtor on Monday about it. I thought about it, and I told him that I had to pray about it first. He looked at me funny and nodded. You see, he doesn't believe as I do yet, but Acts 16:31 says, "If anyone believes on the Lord Jesus Christ, he and his household will be saved." Tommy is part of my household, and I trust and believe that he will be saved. Anyway, I prayed that night, and the Holy Spirit told me to put a "Fleece" out concerning the house. Now, if you don't know what a "Fleece" is, then let me tell you. I believe that for any major decision, like a car purchase, a job, a marriage, or a house, a "Fleece" should be placed in order to make God's choice and not be deceived by the Enemy. So, you say, "What is a Fleece?" well, back in the book of Judges, an Angel came to Gideon while he was hiding from a battle. The Angel of the Lord called him a Mighty Man of Valor. He was anything but and told the Angel so, but the Angel told him that he was going to lead an army against the Midianites and win. Gideon still did not believe him, so he asked the Angel to prove that God would really be with him. He told the Angel that if he took a fleece (old school for blanket); and put it out that night, and if the dew only got on the fleece and not on the grass, then he would believe him. The next morning, he got up, and the fleece was wet with dew, and the grass was dry. He went a step further and said that he still was unsure, he asked to put the fleece out that night, and the dew would get on the grass but not on the fleece. The next morning the fleece was dry, but the grass was wet with dew. He then believed that God would support and be with him. When I put out a fleece, I only need to do it once. So, my fleece to God was that the house would already be under contract and off the market if this were not God's awesome amazing house for us. When I called the realtor the next morning at 9 am, she informed me that it was under contract and not available. Isn't God amazing!!!! He wants only the best for us and wants to be included in all of our decisions. I told Tommy, and he was very disappointed, but I knew that my God had something even better picked out just for us. Tommy and his son Scott had been out riding, and they came upon a house nearer to the Country Club; and on my next day off, he, Nana, and I went out to look at it. I loved it!!! We called the realtor and set up a time to go in. On the day that we went to see it, I prayed that this would be the one. When I walked in the front door, I knew that this was the one. Sometimes you just know that this is God's gift for you. I was so excited, like a kid on Christmas day. Everywhere I went was just perfect and amazing. It was huge. It was double the house that we had in Greensboro. It had a garage and an attached carport at the top of the driveway. It also had a very large and level backyard that would be perfect for the puppy that I had always wanted. It was truly God's awesome amazing house picked out just by Him. I knew that this was the one!!

What's even more amazing was that I had prayed for a new washer and dryer with a slot for the scented fabric softener. The ones at the apartment were from the '70s and were awful. There was a brand-new stackable washer and dryer in the unfinished part of the basement. In the finished part of the basement was a pool table that was really nice, and I also asked for any other furniture, like bedroom suits and the dining room furniture. I asked the realtor if these items could be part of the sale price, and she said that she would ask. The realtor got back in touch with us and said that the owner accepted our offer. WooooHoooooo!!!!!. We were so very excited. We went to the bank and applied for the loan, and then we had to wait. Oh, how awful the waiting was.

The homeowner accepted our offer, and while awaiting our loan to be approved, we would drive by our house almost daily. Some days we would look in the windows to see if they had removed any furniture. I gave away most of the furniture at the apartment, knowing that they would leave everything that God wanted them to. Finally, toward the end of August, we closed on the house. It was on a Friday, and we moved in that night. We just couldn't wait to make it ours. Our realtor company had a moving truck that we could use, and we packed it up and brought what I had not given away.

By the time we had unpacked everything, we were exhausted. They had left the pool table, 3-bedroom sets, a fully furnished dining room, kitchen table with chairs, and the brand-new washer and dryer. Isn't God amazing? Our house was across the street from the Smith River, and they sold us the lot for $25.00-Icing on the cake. We bought the rest of the furniture with cash as we went along, and on December 10th, 2013, I had a housewarming party to show all of my Church Family what God had done for us. My Mom had passed away from lung cancer in May of 2011. She had left $125,000.00 to me to be given out $25,000.00 over the next 5 years, and by the end of 2017, my house was paid off with cash by God, just like He said. God had returned double back what the locusts had stolen.

I continued to flourish at Mercy Crossing and at the Hospital. I loved my "God job" and became fully engaged at the Hospital. I was on many committees and loved precepting New Graduates, and I found that my nursing

"Gift from God" was "End of Life" care. My dad had been on a ventilator and went into a brain fever, and his temperature went up to 108. Alcoholism had been the cause of his illness. He had always said that he did not want to be kept alive on a ventilator and my mother and brother met with an ethics board to make him a DNR and make him comfortable. He struggled for 2 weeks and then finally passed away. My mother was diagnosed with small cell lung cancer and only survived for 5 months with chemotherapy, so I truly could empathize with my patients and family members. I have a heart for these people. By the time for the end-of-life questions, the patient normally cannot make this decision, and it is up to a family member to be their advocate. This is a very delicate situation and conversation, but because of my empathy, I can help to make it a peaceful and joyful time. That is when you truly know that it is a gift from God. Of course, I pray before I have this conversation, and I pray with the family. My first question to the family is, "Do they know Jesus?" if they do, then all the better; but if there is doubt, I pray the "Sinner's Prayer" with the family for the patient. You see, I have asked the Holy Spirit to teach me how to pray perfect will prayers. I believe that when I pray in God's perfect will, He always answers my prayers. How could it be that He would not want all of His children to come home and be with Him? I believe that hearing remains with the patient until he dies. Of course, it is up to each individual to accept Jesus Christ as his Lord and Savior, but I trust and believe that after we pray, they do. This, in turn, gives the family peace and joy that others do not understand. Not everyone understands this, but I believe that I will see these people when I get to Heaven.

Covid hit in 2020 and knocked the breath out of all my team. I have an AWESOME team, managers, and "O" s. My job was truly hand-picked by God. We come to work daily for the express purpose of making someone better. We love what we do and take great pride in it. Covid is a man-made virus that is illogical and evil. As CCU nurses, we are always trying to figure out what is going on so that we can fix it or help family members to let go. By the time people with Covid made it to CCU, they were pretty much done. We worked and turned and medicated and ventilated, but mostly to no avail. When families were not allowed in and their loved ones were dying, we stayed in the room and held their hands. We let no one die alone. It was very hard. I made a point to call my family member twice a day at set times to update and answer questions. I am very empathetic, but I am also very blunt. I try not to give false hope. I would rather prepare their heart and mind for the worst, and if things get better, then wonderful. Anyway, I had a young man in his 40s, and I would call his wife twice a day and update her. I would pray with her, and we would pray for him, but he, too, eventually died. It was just so very hard. But amazingly, she told me that she was a nurse and that my care for her and her husband had made a difference in her life and her practice. She called my hospital and asked that I be given the 'Daisy Award.' I was not aware of this and had never heard about this award, but on February 12, 2021, I came into work like any other day and was lovingly surprised with the presentation of my hospital's 1st Daisy Award.

Danielle McClain Henderson, the nurse and family member who nominated me, was also allowed to be there. I got the best hug and have a sister in Christ and a friend for life. This was an amazing award and is ALL God. Without Jesus, this day never would have happened. I would

probably be dead and in hell. You see, without this car wreck, I would not have come to know Jesus Christ. The Holy Spirit told me that on that day back in 2003 that Satan had planned on killing me and taking me to hell; but God had been rubbing his hands together in excited anticipation, thinking, "Devil, you just don't know what you are getting ready to start." All of this is thanks to Mrs.___ and I will be eternally grateful to be a 'Crown' for her and look forward to the day that I get to meet her in heaven and give her a hug. I am no longer ashamed of my past and who I was. I am a princess, and my Dad's a King. 2 Corinthians 5:17(NLT) says, "This means that anyone who belongs to Christ, has become a new person. The old life is gone; a new life has begun." My past no longer controls me. Jesus gave me a choice, and I will praise Him and talk about Him and thank Him for eternity.

I AM A NEW CREATION

MORNING LIFE VERSES

Good morning, Lord. I sure do love You.

- I give you my will so that I may do Yours. Ps 143:10
- Create in me a clean heart and renew a steadfast spirit in me. Ps 51:10
- May the words of my mouth and the meditations of my heart be pleasing in your sight. Ps 19:14
- I'm called to be the head and not the tail, above and not beneath. Deuteronomy 28:13 To be in wellness, not in illness, to be able to lend and not have to borrow, to be blessed so that I may not be cursed.
- I am like a tree, planted by streams of living water, which bears its fruit in due season; its leaves do not whither, and everything that it does prospers. Ps 1:3
- You are my portion and my cup of blessing. Ps 16:5
- You hold my future in Your right hand, and the boundary lines have fallen into pleasant places for me. I have a beautiful inheritance, and I will not be

shaken. I will keep you in mind at all times. Ps 16:5-8

- Therefore, be gracious to me, oh Lord, according to Your faithful love, according to Your abundant mercy, blot out my rebellion. Ps 51:1

- Let the words of my mouth be Yours and not mine; may the thoughts that I think be Yours and not mine, and let the actions that I do be Yours and not mine. Ps 19:14

- I believe Lord Jesus, help my unbelief. Help me to understand, realize and walk in that 100-fold faith that You have for me. Mark 9:24

- I'll eat what you want me to eat, I'll look like You want me to look, and I'll weigh what You want me to weigh. 1st Timothy 4:4

- I'll understand, remember and excel in all that I learn today. Ps 32:8

- I look forward to this day, Lord, with hopeful and excited expectation, knowing that You are going to use me. Always handpick my patients and the people that I come into contact with. Philippians 1:20

- I put on the Full Armor of God: I put on the Breastplate of Righteousness; so that I may have a Christ-like heart. I put on the Girdle of Truth; so that You may give me words of wisdom, knowledge, and understanding. I put on the Shoes of Peace; so that I may be a peacemaker and spread the Good News. I put on the Helmet of Salvation; so that I may have Christ-like thoughts. I put on the Shield of Faith; so that I may repel the fiery darts that Satan throws my way; and I put on the Sword of the Spirit, the 2-edged sword; so that I may fight the enemy with Your word and so that You may convict me when I am wrong. I am now fully armed with the Full Armor of God, and I am prepared for victory today.

  Ephesians 6:11

ALWAYS SPEAK LIFE- NOT DEATH!!!

Made in United States
North Haven, CT
13 November 2022